ADVANCED PLACEMENT
STUDENT COMPANION

to accompany

Human Geography
Culture, Society, and Space

Sixth Edition

H. J. de Blij
Marshall University

Alexander B. Murphy
University of Oregon

with references to
Human Geography in Action

Michael Kuby
Arizona State University

John Harner
University of Colorado at Colorado Springs

Patricia Gober
Arizona State University

includes

Study Guide

James F. Marran, Social Studies Chair Emeritus
New Trier Township High School
Winnetka, Illinois

Take Note!
Art Notebook

Virtual Field Guide

Margaret M. Gripshover
Marshall University

Glenn R. Miller
Bridgewater State College

Website access card

John Wiley & Sons, Inc.

New York • Chichester • Weinheim • Brisbane • Singapore • Toronto

COVER PHOTO: Gary John Norman/Tony Stone Images

To order books or for customer service call 1-800-CALL-WILEY (225-5945).

ISBN 0-471-35559-3

Printed in the United States of America

10 9 8 7 6 5 4 3 2 1

Printed and bound by Courier Kendallville, Inc.

Table of Contents

Web access card

If the identification number has expired or the Web access card is missing, please call People's Publishing Group at 800-822-1080.

STUDY GUIDE

Introduction

Using the Study Guide

The **Study Guide** is a tool for students preparing to take the Advanced Placement Human Geography examination as a result of using *Human Geography: Culture, Society, and Space* (Sixth Edition). It is organized to provide not only strategies for using the text but also to present a comprehensive introduction to the Advanced Placement Program and information about the end-of course testing program available to students each May.

First and foremost, Advanced Placement Human Geography is a college-level program that goes well beyond the memorization of facts and the simple recall of details. Students are expected to use thinking skills that require comprehension, application, analysis, evaluation, and synthesis. Indeed this is no small order. They must not only master the basic information in the course in Human Geography, but also understand the concepts, trends and relations that give that information meaning. This makes it useful in interpreting the topics that define the Advanced Placement Human Geography course. There are seven such topics that provide the course framework. They are: Human Geography - Its Nature and Perspectives, Population, Cultural Patterns and Processes, Political organization of Space, Agriculture and Rural land Use, Industrialization and Economic Development, and Cities and Urban Land Use.

Because Advanced Placement Human Geography is a college-level course, it is directed at meeting these five goals that complement *Geography for Life: National Geography Standards* (1994) and characterize the objectives of the introductory college course in human geography:

1. to understand and use maps and spatial data sets;
2. to understand and interpret the implications of associations among phenomena in places;
3. to recognize and interpret at different scales the relationships among patterns and processes;
4. to define regions and evaluate the regionalization process;
5. to describe and analyze changing interconnections among places.

Unlike high school textbooks in geography, college texts expect students to assume greater responsibility for their own learning. As a result, college books have fewer study helps and prompts, fewer review questions, and fewer end-of-chapter review sections with attendant exercises such as writing activities and independent study projects. *Human Geography: Culture, Society, and Space* (Sixth Edition) is no exception. It is a straightforward expository development of the complexity of human geography using field notes, case studies, photographs, maps and other graphics to achieve its purpose. In addition, to help students understand the utilitarian aspects of human geography, each chapter concludes with "Applying Geographic Knowledge." This section poses two problem-based challenges requiring students to use what they have learned to develop solutions.

The **Study Guide** has been prepared to help students make the successful transition from a high school course which is almost always teacher-directed to a college course which places the responsibility for learning squarely on the learners. It will assist students in understanding how to master more material in greater depth and with broader implications than has been their experience in most of their high school courses. While Advanced Placement Human Geography as an academic disciple is predicated on theories and concepts about human activities across Earth's surface, its real value is in its utilitarian applications. While *Human Geography: Culture, Society, and Space* (Sixth Edition) is rich with examples illustrating the uses of human geography, the **Study Guide** provides direction for students in the application of its theories and concepts. This is especially helpful when answering the kind of multiple-choice and free-response questions they will encounter on the Advanced Placement Human Geography examination. The pre-test questions in Chapter 4 provide apt examples of the breadth and variety of questions students can expect on the Advanced Placement Human Geography end-of-course test.

Students should recognize that the **Study Guide** is not a substitute for the text. It will facilitate its use and should be utilized in combination with it. Further, referring to appropriate sections of *Human Geography in Action* (Wiley, 1998) as cited in the **Study Guide** will also help students see the relationship between the "big ideas" developed in the text and their application. This hands-on book contains activities (many computer-based) that encourage students to learn geography by doing geography.

The opening chapters of the **Study Guide** introduce students to the Advanced Placement Program, explain what human geography is, and provide some basic information about the Advanced Placement Human Geography examination with a variety of sample questions. The format for the remaining chapters which provide a guide to the seven topics in the course outline is the same. Each begins with a brief essay defining the dimensions of the topic and its place in human geography. This is a context essay and should be read before studying the sections relating to the topic in the textbook. The remaining elements of the chapter are:

- Focus question to direct topic inquiry
- Key word/definitions
- Topic outline/text correlations
- Topic study questions
- Researching the topic
- Connecting to *Human Geography in Action*
- Sample multiple choice questions
- Sample free-response questions

Because each teacher will approach Advanced Placement Human Geography using a different organizational format and a variety of different teaching strategies, students should recognize that the **Study Guide** might not precisely complement their teacher's style. However, the components of *Human Geography: Culture, Society, and Space* (Sixth Edition) will enhance mastery of the content of human geography and prepare students for taking the Advanced Placement examination. The multiple-choice and free-response questions will be especially helpful in providing a model for the examination.

Additional Suggestions for Student Strategies for Course Preparation

1. Keep a set of comprehensive notes on classes in Advanced Placement Human Geography and use them as an integral part of the study regimen.

2. Maintain a personal glossary of terms beyond those suggested in the guide. A significant part of effective preparation for the Advanced Placement examination is vocabulary building.

3. Consider organizing a study group with three or four classmates. The group should meet regularly (at least twice a week and before every test) to compare notes, define key words, raise questions, clarify information, and provide mutual support.

4. Have a detailed and current world atlas at the ready as a reference for locational analysis issues and questions about absolute and relative location, site, and situation.

5. Check the College Board website every several weeks for any updates on Advanced Placement Human Geography and other matters relating to Advanced Placement. The site is: www.collegeboard.org.

6. Maintain a folio of work to serve not only as a record of what has been accomplished (i.e., research papers, special projects, quizzes, tests, etc.), but also as a resource to help review the Advanced Placement Human Geography curriculum in the days immediately prior to the May examination.

Chapter 1

Understanding Advanced Placement

What is the Advanced Placement (AP) Program?

AP is a program of college level courses and examinations that gives high school students the opportunity to receive advanced placement and/or credit when they enter college. The courses and exams reflect the content and goals of a first-year college course that is offered and widely accepted by a large number of college and university departments in the discipline.

The Advanced Placement Program is administered and managed by the College Board, the same organization that offers the Scholastic Aptitude Test (SAT) and the Preliminary Scholastic Aptitude Test (PSAT) each year.

How many students are involved?

In 1998, some 600,000 students in more than 14,000 high schools worldwide took nearly one million AP exams. About 2,900 colleges and universities grant credit, advanced placement, or both to students who have performed satisfactorily on the exams. Some students receive sophomore standing when they have demonstrated competence in three or more of the exams.

How can a student participate in Advanced Placement in preparation for the end-of-course examination?

- through a prescribed Advanced Placement course
- through an intensive regular high school course program (typically at the honors level)
- through a tutorial
- through independent study

What courses are presently offered in the AP program?

The Advanced Placement Program consists of 33 college-level courses and exams in 19 disciplines

Art: History of Art, Studio Art (Drawing and General)
Biology
Calculus: AB, BC
Chemistry
Computer Science: A* and AB
Economics: Macroeconomics*, Microeconomics*
English: English Language and Composition, English Literature and Composition, and International English Language
Environmental Science*
French: French Language, French Literature
Geography: Human**
German Language
Government and Politics: Comparative*, United States*
History: European, United States
Latin: Literature, Vergil
Music Theory
Physics: B, C: Electricity and Magnetism*, C: Mechanics*

Psychology*
Spanish: Language, Literature
Statistics*

* Subjects marked with an asterisk are the equivalent of half-year (or semester) college courses. The others are year-long (or two semesters) college courses.

** Human Geography is the most recent addition. World History is in the planning stage and will be included within the next few years.

What is the format of an Advanced Placement exam?

All AP exams contain both multiple-choice and free-response questions. The latter require essay writing, problem solving and the use of a number of critical thinking skills. The multiple-choice section accounts for half of the student's examination grade and the free-response section for the other half.

How are the exams graded?

Multiple-choice questions are machine scored.

Free-response questions are scored by about 2,300 college professors and high school Advanced Placement teachers who meet together in teams for one week in June at various college venues in the United States. Team members evaluate individual student answers using a carefully developed set of criteria. Team leaders do frequent cross checks to assure validity and consistency in grading.

Each exam receives a grade on a five-point scale:
5   extremely well qualified
4   well qualified
3   qualified
2   possibly qualified
1   no recommendation

How can a student receive special recognition for performing well on an Advanced Placement exam?

For a number of years, the College Board has recognized AP students who earn grades of 3 or higher on at least three full-year AP examinations or the equivalent number of half-year courses. Such students receive the Advanced Placement Scholar Award.

Is there an Advanced Placement Diploma?

Presently there is no special diploma for AP students but the College Board is conducting a pilot study to determine the feasibility of awarding such a diploma. If the study is a success, the Advanced Placement Diploma will be available for students who quality in the 2001-2002 school year. To earn a diploma, students will be expected to take five Advanced Placement courses and earn a 3 or better on each test. At this point, however, the AP Diploma Project is still very much a work in progress with the prerequisites subject to change.

Why has geography been established as an Advanced Placement subject?

Geography addresses a number of important and wide-ranging questions from issues dealing with climate change to ethnic conflict to urban sprawl. A growing number of scholars in other disciplines realize that it is a mistake to treat all places as if they were essentially the same, or to undertake research on an environment that does not include an examination of the relationship between human and physical processes in the various regions of the world. Understanding such interactions in an increasing globalized society affirms the importance of geography as yet another tool students can use to inform their world view.

What kind of geography is included in the Advanced Placement program?

It is a college-level course the equivalent of a semester's introductory college course in Human Geography. The course is structured to address human geography's seven core topics: the nature of geography, population, cultural patterns and processes, the political organization of space, agricultural and rural land use, industrial and economic development, and cities and urban land use.

What is Human Geography?

Quite simply, it is the study of people from a spatial and ecological perspective. People are central to geography in that their activities help shape Earth's surface largely through their interaction with the physical environment. Human settlements and structures are part of that tapestry of interaction. It is in that milieu that humans either compete for control of space and resources or work out systems of social, economic and political cooperation.

How is the Advanced Placement Human Geography course organized?

There are seven topics in the program. Each is presented as a separate unit of study. Here is the outline used to develop the Advanced Placement examination. It reflects the structure of the typical introductory human geography course at the college level and is likely to be the outline Advanced Placement teachers will be using with their classes. The **Study Guide** for *Human Geography; Culture, Society, and Space* (Sixth Edition) is also organized to address these topics. The following is the summary outline.

Advanced Placement Human Geography

Course Outline

I. Geography: Its Nature and Perspectives*
    • Geography as a field of inquiry
    • Evolution of key geographical concepts and models associated with notable geographers
    • Key concepts underlying the geographical perspective: space, place, and scale
    • Key geographical skills
    • Sources of geographical ideas and data: the field, census data, etc.

II. Population°
    • Geographical analysis of population
    • Population distribution and composition
    • Population growth and decline over time and space
    • Population movement

III.   Cultural Patterns and Processes°
- Concept of culture
- Cultural differences
- Environmental impact of cultural attitudes and practices
- Cultural landscapes and cultural identity

IV.   Political Organization of Space°
- Nature and significance of political boundaries
- Evolution of the contemporary political pattern
- Challenges to inherited political-territorial arrangements

V.   Agricultural and Rural Land Use°
- Development and diffusion of agriculture
- Major agricultural production regions
- Rural land use and change
- Impacts of modern agriculture

VI.   Industrial and Economic Development°
- Character of industrialization
- Spatial aspects of the rise of industrial economies
- Contemporary global patterns of industrialization/ resource extraction
- Impacts of industrialization

VII.   Cities and Urban Land Use°
- Definition of urbanization
- Origin and evolution of cities
- Functional character of contemporary cities
- Built environment and social space
- Responses to urban growth

* Topic constitutes 6%-8% of the course.
° Topic constitutes 15%-17% of the course.

Is there an Advanced Placement website?

Further information about the AP Program is available at

www.collegeboard.org/ap

Is there an "official" publication explaining Advanced Placement Human Geography?

As with all Advanced Placement programs, the College Board publishes a course description. The one available for Human Geography is the May, 1999 <u>Preliminary Edition</u>. Copies are available through the College Board regional offices or by contacting the College Board directly. The standard print version of the booklet with complete information about the Advanced Placement Human Geography course will be available in the spring of 2000.
A number of other publications are also available to help students and their parents learn more about Advanced Placement and the courses and exams that are available. Many items can be ordered on line through the AP Aisle of the College Board Online store at http://cbweb2.collegeboard.org.shopping/. Alternatively, publications are available through AP Order Services at 609-771-7243.

Chapter 2

Defining Geography: What Is It? What Does It Mean?

Note to the student: When you finish reading this essay, you should be able to do two things:
- describe geography in a single paragraph;
- explain the importance of geography in a three paragraph essay using strong topic sentences to introduce each paragraph and incorporating the key words listed below in the body of the essay.

Key Words: geography   spatial   human/physical systems
                     location   place   interaction
                     themes   traditions   environment

Geography as a discipline is confounding. Trying to define it is elusive because it is so imprecise. To understand geography is not necessarily to know what it is. Instead it is to understand what it encompasses. As a result, geography is more meaningful when it is described rather than when it is defined.

Many people perceive geography as simply an exercise in place location. That means being able to answer a single question about a place: Where is it? If, for example, Chicago is identified as a city in northeastern Illinois on the southwestern shore of Lake Michigan, that information has indeed answered the "Where is it?" question. To be even more accurate, data on the city's latitudinal and longitudinal coordinates could be given showing it at 41°49'N, 87°37'W.

Even though such identifiers about Chicago's location are accurate, they bring the inquirer only to the threshold of really getting the total "geographic" picture because there are other more important and more interesting questions to pose and answer about places. Chicago becomes far more meaningful when it is understood in the context of the answers to these questions:

- Why is it where it is?
- How did it get there?
- What does it look like?
- Where is it in relation to other places?
- Why is it important?
- How is it connected to other places in its region, its country, its continent, and the world?
- How does it interact with other places?

Learning the answers to these questions begins to give Chicago dimension and meaning since they identify both its physical (natural) and human (cultural) features. They also provide a context for studying the spatial characteristics of the city by making clear both its site (i.e., its physical setting) and its situation (i.e., its location in relation to other places). More importantly, the interaction between Chicago's physical and cultural features help explain its role as an immensely diverse urban magnet that for almost two centuries has drawn people from across the world to live and work in its neighborhoods and the hinterland beyond. Photographs and maps showing the tracks that lace the city's rail yards like so many scrimshaw etchings and the mile-long runways accommodating thousands of flights daily at O'Hare International Airport reveal a tapestry of transportation networks moving people, goods, ideas, and services to and from all corners of Earth. And the communications aerials atop Sears Tower and the Hancock Building in the central business district (CBD) send images and words that inform, entertain, and challenge people around the globe. As a manufacturing core and marketplace for making most of the world's candy and wholesaling everything from elegant silks to finished steel for bridges and buildings, Chicago provides a commercial function that helps make the economy of the United States the world's largest and strongest.

Certainly a list inventorying the city's role that derives from its location could go on and on, but the point is clear. Wherever a place is only marks the beginning of giving it definition and establishing its importance among other places. By examining the spatial aspects of a place's location and how the people living there function and make their livings confirm that geography is not so much about the memorization of facts but about asking questions, solving problems, and making informed decisions about the physical and human complexities of the planet.

More than anything else, geography is an integrative disciple That is why it is so difficult to define. It brings together the physical and human systems of the world in the study of people, places, and environments.

Human Geography: Culture, Society, and Space (Sixth Edition) provides some valuable insights in the two introductory sections of chapter 1 about the meaning, traditions, and themes of geography (pp. 2-7). The chapter's introductory sentence serves as an appropriate point of departure for the study of the Advanced Placement program in Human Geography. "Geography is destiny," the authors assert, and proceed through the book's development to describe how exactly this is so. In the course of study, geography is portrayed as making its subject matter Earth's surface and the systems that shape it, the relationships existing between people and their environments, and the connections between people and the place where they live, work, play, and visit. It becomes the process of knowing and understanding spatial interaction. Ultimately, as a special habit of mind, geography is a way of thinking about the world and its people through the prism of place and space.

Chapter 3

The Vocabulary of Advanced Placement: Prepping to be a Successful Test-Taker

All Advanced Placement courses are designed to prepare students for the examinations offered each May. That means learning for the test to earn the best possible score is central to the Advanced Placement experience. Effective test-taking is just as much a skill as using a textbook efficiently, or writing a comprehensive and well-organized research essay, or learning the vocabulary specific to a subject. Thus developing strategies to do well on the Advanced Placement Human Geography test is as important as knowing and understanding the content of the program of study itself.

Free-Response Questions

Students will have a prescribed amount of time to plan and write at least three essays in the free-response section of the Advanced Placement Human Geography exam. Therefore, it is essential that they not only manage their time well but also answer the questions asked as precisely and fully as possible. To do that, having a clear understanding of the meaning of the "operative" action verb will simplify the development of each essay. Being able to recall information is certainly important, but more important is understanding what the question is asking. If, for example, a question indicates that you are to **evaluate** some aspect of human geography and you proceed only to **describe** it, then you have missed the point. Remember that an essay must directly answer the question asked. Thus student responses must be pointed and precise.

The seven verbs defined below represent key terms used on Advanced Placement exams. Sample question in human geography follow each definition. The notation in brackets refers to sections in *Human Geography: Culture, Society, and Space* (Sixth Edition) that provide information for preparing substantive answers.

1. **Analyze**: determine the component parts; examine the nature and relationship.

Analyze the spatial relationships between land values and prominent urban features (e.g., central business districts, open spaces near public parks, industrial sites hotels and office development near an international airport). {Chapter 22, 292-301. Incorporate information about Weber's industrial location theory (296) as well as the von Thüen model (200, 296). Include information about least cost theory (295).}

2. **Assess/Evaluate:** judge the value or character of something; evaluate the positive and negative points; give an opinion regarding the value of something.

Evaluate the advantages and disadvantages of allowing foreign-owned businesses to purchase land, open factories or conduct other kinds of business in a host country. {Use information from urban geography, especially chapter 18 (238-52). Also include information about globalization trends (270, 503). Note, too the relationship between trade and culture (136-7).}

3. **Compare**: examine for the purposes of noting similarities and differences.

Compare the geographic effects of migration streams and counter-streams of rural African Americans to northern urban centers earlier in the 20th century to those of the Irish who emigrated to the United States after the Potato Famine in 1848. {Note the difference between external migrations (96-100) and internal migrations (100-4). Show the applications of expansion diffusion and relocation diffusion as they apply to both the African

American and Irish experiences (26-7). Address the issue of the geography of dislocation when developing your answer (84-6).}

4. **Contrast**: examine to show dissimilarities or points of difference.

Contrast the attitudes toward resource development and use by 19th century entrepreneurs and 20th century conservationists. {Use information in Chapter 21, (282-91), especially section on "Concepts and Approaches" (284-7). Refer also to "Understanding Environmental Change" (471-6).}

5. **Describe**: give an account of; tell about; provide a word picture.

Using the photographs on 238, 251, 253, and 255 of *Human Geography: Culture, Society, and Space* (Sixth Edition), describe what these cityscapes reveal about the pattern and structure of the modern city. {Refer to Chapter 19, especially "Urban Spatial Structure" (256-8).}

6. **Discuss**: talk over; write about; consider or examine from various points of view; debate; present the various sides of the issue.

Discuss the importance of the emerging supranational organizations (e.g., United Nations, European Union, Organization of African Unity, etc.) as political and economic expressions of new frameworks for dealing with such international issues as population policy, settling boundary disputes, and relocating refugees and other displaced people. {Use the information in Chapter 27 (368-82). Note especially the section on "Regional Multinational Unions" (375- 81).}

7. **Explain**: make clear; provide the causes or reasons for something; make known in detail; tell the meaning of.

Explain how voluntary international migrations are shaped by push and pull factors. {Focus on "Theories of Migration" (83) and "Push and Pull Factors" (83-4).}

Multiple-Choice Questions

Typically there are 80 questions in the multiple-choice section of the Advanced Placement history/social science examinations (including human geography). The difficulty is intentionally set at such a level that a candidate has to answer 50 to 60 percent of the questions correctly to receive a 3. Random guessing is discouraged, but students having some knowledge of the question and who can eliminate one or more choices and then select what they reason to be the best answer from the remaining choices, are likely to have some success. But the key to performing well on a multiple choice test is to read each question carefully in order to understand its purpose and connect it to what has been learned in the study of human geography.

Questions are distributed among the topics that define the course of studies in human geography as well as the concepts fundamental to understanding the principles of the discipline. Since geographers use models to replicate, explain, and predict reality, it is important to know what such models are and the theories that serve as the hypotheses on which they are based.

The questions included here are examples of the kinds that typically appear on Advanced Placement exams in history and the social sciences. They represent categories that range from being able to recognize specific data in some detail to more sophisticated analytical questions, including those challenging students to differentiate among conflicting causes and their effects. The most challenging questions are those that call for interpretation and evaluation.

Recall: These are fact-based questions that require students to recollect specific information.

1. A unique form of rural settlement developed in French Canada is known as
    A. long lots.
    B. village centered agriculture.
    C. riverside communes.
    D. township and range segments.
    E. extended homesteads.

2. People who practice slash and burn agriculture make their living as
    A. subsistence farmers.
    B. nomadic herders.
    C. hunters and gatherers.
    D. guest workers.
    E. stateless migrants.

Determining Cause: The word "because" is always a part of the stem in this category of question. The student is expected to identify a reason for something.

3. The Brazilian economy prospered in the 1960s and early 1970s but in the decade that followed, it suffered a significant collapse because
    A. there was a fall in the price of coffee.
    B. the country amassed a staggering foreign debt.
    C. the cost of imported fuel escalated.
    D. the democratic government was overthrown.
    E. development was concentrated in the Atlantic coastal cities.

4. The geographer Ellsworth Huntington believed that certain civilizations were more advanced than others because of
    A. irredentism.
    B. chance breakthroughs.
    C. the overall accessibility of certain world regions.
    D. climate factors.
    E. transculturation.

Interpreting Maps and Other Graphics: Students are provided a visual prompt that they must analyze and then identify the correct answer. Questions 5 and 6 require analysis and interpretation of a table, diagram, and map. Each is referenced to a graphic in *Human Geography: Culture, Society, and Space* (Sixth Edition) on the page identified in the body of the question.

5. Using Table 21-1 (Per Capita GNP) on 283, what reservation is an economic geographer likely to express about the economies of the countries listed after studying the data?

    A. The data do not reveal any of the details about national economies.

    B. Only the GNPs of very poor and very rich countries are provided.

    C. With the availability of more sophisticated data, GNP information is no longer a helpful tool in economic analysis.

    D. The table provides information too selective to be of any value in predicting a nation's economic strength.

    E. The table presents no information about the variations and inequities within the economies of the nations listed regardless of how strong or weak they are.

6. What is the purpose of Figure 19-3 on 259?

    A. to show the nesting of regions within regions in terms of their importance

    B. to show patterns of development on the rural landscape

    C. to indicate that only selected central places serve vital functions

    D. to illustrate how metropolitan areas are connected

    E. to provide information predicting a region's growth potential

Except Questions: AP multiple choice questions are never framed using negatives (i.e., Which of the following is <u>not</u> an example of cultural assimilation?). Rather the stem contains "except" as a way of having students discriminate among the possible responses.

7. All of the following have typically been true of plantation agriculture in Middle America except:

    A. It produces crops for export.

    B. It is an inefficient operation.

    C. It produces only a single crop.

    D. The capital and skills necessary to support it are imported.

    E. Labor on the plantations is seasonal.

8. All of these are rural economic activities presently operating in Eastern Colorado except

    A. cattle ranching.

    B. wheat farming.

    C. horse breeding.

    D. dude ranching.

    E. corn growing.

Effects: This is a modification of the recall type question except that the student is challenged to identify <u>why</u> some phenomenon occurs.

9. In human geography, the process of expansion diffusion involves

    A. the spread of some innovation by a migrating people.

    B. the development of culture hearths in different places at different times.

    C. the use of innovation waves in controlling the movement of refugees.

    D. an innovation wave meeting with an absorbing barrier.

    E. the movement of a new idea or technology through an established and fixed population.

10. In an analysis of demographic transition, which of these sequences fails to complement the model?
    A. Stage 1: high birth rate and high death rate
    B. Stage 4: low birth rate and low death rate
    C. Stage 2: high death rate and low birth rate
    D. Stage 3: low population growth rate
    E. Stage 1: low population growth rate

True/False: From a series of statements or phrases, the student selects the one that is accurate/wrong. Very often such questions are variations on recall-type inquiries because they expect students to identify information they have memorized.

11. How are people identified who are forced to move from their homes to relocation camps in another country because of civil war or some governmental malfunction?
    A. prisoners of war
    B. internal migrants
    C. political refugees
    D. migrant workers
    E. displaced persons

12. Which of the following statements about Rotterdam, The Netherlands is the only accurate one?
    A. It. is located on the Volga River.
    B. It is the headquarters of the North Atlantic Treaty Organization.
    C. It is the world's busiest port city.
    D. It is the gateway to the Baltic Sea.
    E. It is Western Europe's largest city.

Analyzing a Statement: This type of question is a test of reading skills. The student is given a statement several sentences in length and is asked to interpret it.

13. Puerto Rico stands in sharp contrast to Hispanola and Jamaica, its closest western neighbors. Long dependent on a single crop economy (sugar), Puerto Rico during the 1950s and 1960s industrialized rapidly as a result of tax breaks for corporations, relatively cheap labor, various kinds of government incentives, political stability, and special access to the markets in the United States. As a result, today, chemicals and pharmaceuticals - not sugar - rank as the leading exports.

The description provided here is most characteristic of
    A. a command economy.
    B. economic imperialism.
    C. centralized planning.
    D. a market economy.
    E. postindustrial investment

14. In order to ensure the island's continued economic success, a geographic analyst might likely recommend that it
    A. reintroduce large-scale sugar cultivation.
    B. begin to plan for large-scale banana production.
    C. seek independence from the United States.
    D. initiate a comprehensive long-range plan for economic development.
    E. develop an economic union with Jamaica and the countries on Hispanola.

Answers: 1. A 2. A 3. C; 4. D 5. E 6. A 7. B 8. E 9. E 10. C 11. C 12. C 13. D
14. D

Chapter 4

Advanced Placement Pre-Test in Human Geography

The following are examples of the kinds of multiple-choice and free-response questions on the Advanced Placement examination in Human Geography. The distribution of topics as cited in the answer section to the test in this chapter and the level of difficulty are illustrative of the composition of the examination.

Before students begin the course in Advanced Placement Human Geography, they should take this pre-test to assess their level of competence.

Multiple-Choice Questions

Directions: Each of the questions or incomplete statements is followed by five suggested answers or completions. Select the one that is best in each case.

1. In the rapidly growing cities of the developing world, the areas where the poorest migrants from rural areas tend to settle are
    A. in slums surrounding the central city.
    B. in squatter settlements on the outskirts of the city.
    C. in the commercial sector.
    D. adjacent to shopping malls and discount outlets.
    E. near places of employment.

2. When people identify the "old neighborhood" as the place where they grew up, which of these kinds of geographic features are they primarily identifying?
    A. geologic
    B. systematic
    C. agrarian
    D. physical
    E. cultural

3. A forward city is a city strategically placed by a national government to identify some aspect of a country's goal for either internal development or for establishing a position of importance in the international community. Which of these cities best represents a forward capital in the modern world?
    A. Beijing
    B. Brasilia
    C. Washington, D.C.
    D. Cairo
    E. Berlin

4. An appropriate geographic synonym for the Middle East is
    A. Anatolia.
    B. North Africa.
    C. Trans-Caucasus.
    D. Southwest Asia.
    E. East Asia.

5. Which of these was a "pull factor" that encouraged poor European migrants to settle in the United States in the late 19th century?
    A. compulsory military service for males
    B. civil rights
    C. job opportunities in factories and on farms
    D. use of English as a primary language in the public schools
    E. the promise of citizenship for joining the army

6. What has the "Green Revolution" accomplished since it was implemented in the 1960s?
    A. It has brought an understanding that the world's tropical rainforests are endangered.
    B. It has freed the developing countries in Africa from fear of a food shortage.
    C. It has called attention to the effect of acid rain on forests in industrial regions.
    D. It has greatly increased yields of basic food crops in some developing countries.
    E. It has marked the end of such tropical diseases as malaria.

7. Which of the following is the best example of a transition zone?
    A. The Sahel
    B. Great Lakes Region
    C. Nile River
    D. Appalachian Mountains
    E. San Andreas Fault

8. Which of these is an example of sequent occupance?
    A. Mount Everest
    B. South African veld
    C. Indonesian rainforest
    D. Montana cattle ranch
    E. North Atlantic Drift

9. In which of these ways did the principle of intervening opportunity affect migration to Australia in the early days of settlement on that continent?
    A. Information about Australia flowing back to Britain was blocked by the Pacific Ocean.
    B. European cultural influences were slow to reach Australia.
    C. Many British emigrants settled in colonies closer to England rather than travel the great distance to Australia.
    D. People in England perceived Australia to be so hostile an environment that colonization would never be successful there.
    E. The Australian aborigines made settlement difficult in the interior of the country.

10. Austin, Texas has become a center for the manufacture of computers. What major change has most likely resulted in the economy of the city and its region?
    A. The state government has had to relocate because of the increase in the size of the population.
    B. Fewer minimum wage jobs are available now than a few years ago.
    C. Most of the citizens of Austin have been unaffected by this addition to the city's economy.
    D. The quality of life has diminished because of the influx of the new workers and their families.
    E. There has been a building boom because of the demand for housing for all the new workers and their families.

11. When certain maps identifying the physical features of a place or region include contour lines, their purpose is to show
> A. local boundaries.
> B. differences in elevation.
> C. variations in population densities.
> D. latitude and longitude.
> E. distances between places.

12. What was the major result of the journeys and voyages of Marco Polo and Christopher Columbus?
> A. the development of an international organization to resolve conflicts
> B. the discovery of many new medicines and herbal remedies
> C. an introduction of representative systems of government to areas beyond Europe
> D. decrease in poverty and disease in the world
> E. increase in trade among the world's regions

13. Which of these provides the best description of a culture region?
> A. an area with similar physical characteristics
> B. a section of the world with countries where people of the same race live
> C. an area where the people who live there have been environmentally responsible
> D. a collection of countries whose people practice the same religion and speak a common language
> E. an area historically marked by religious and ethnic conflict

14. "Comparative advantage" is a term in economic geography that refers to a place's ability to produce a product relatively more effectively than another because of its relative location and the resources it possesses. What competitive advantage does Massachusetts have over Illinois?
> A. significant untapped offshore petroleum reserves
> B. a large annual cranberry crop
> C. a small, highly skilled work force
> D. an efficient state government structure
> E. a world-class system of higher education

15. Which of the following is an example of how early African farmers adapted to the physical conditions in the savanna regions between the Sahara Desert and the equatorial rainforest?
> A. The farmers grew the same crops as they had in the coastal regions in North Africa along the Mediterranean Sea, but in smaller quantities.
> B. The farmers planted wind breaks and palm trees to protect and shade the crops.
> C. The farmers used hoes and rakes instead of plows when planting crops to protect the seeds in the dry soil from erosion.
> D. The farmers became nomads because the soil was so poor it could only produce crops for a year of two.
> E. The farmers abandoned crop farming and turned to herding cattle.

16. Study the map of Singapore on 245 in *Human Geography: Culture, Society, and Space* (Sixth Edition). Its purpose is to demonstrate all of the following except
> A. some of the physical characteristics of the region.
> B. the degree of urbanization on Singapore Island.
> C. the relative location of Singapore.
> D, the island's transportation system.
> E. the economic resources available in Singapore.

17. Which of these capital cities was specifically designed to be a national administrative center?
    A. Ottawa
    B. London
    C. Buenos Aries
    D. Tokyo
    E. Pretoria

18. The international "operational" boundary situation most likely to be the subject of dispute between the two countries sharing it is the one
    A defined by a river.
    B. negotiated by a United Nations commission in 1995.
    C. agreed upon by treaty more than a century ago.
    D. fixed by a meridian of longitude.
    E. determined by a time-honored medieval charter.

19. Maria lives in a city of 80,000 people 300 miles from a metropolitan area with a population of 2 million. Which of the following activities would be the most likely reason for Maria to travel to the metropolitan area in her region?
    A. to purchase a new car
    B. to participate in a sales meeting
    C. to attend a major league baseball game
    D. to arrange a bank loan for starting a new business
    E. to attend a four year college

Note: Consider the content of the paragraph below to answer questions 20-21.

On a daily basis, 250,000 people are added to Earth's population. Most are born into nations in the developing world. Tragically, that means that one person in five lives in absolute poverty. One of the results of such deprivation is that almost one billion people in today's world can neither read nor write, and the numbers are growing. As a result, they are forced to live in subsistence economies.

20. Based on the information in the above paragraph, what is a characteristic of the developing world?
    A. low birthrates
    B. stable infant mortality rates
    C. moderate fertility rates
    D. low rates of literacy
    E. stable political conditions

21. This paragraph describes conditions relating to
    A. population distribution.
    B. political structures.
    C. demographic characteristics.
    D. cultural features.
    E. relative location.

22. Which of the following contains the essential components for a well-integrated state?
    A. It has a well developed primary core area and a mature capital city.
    B. It has a federal system of government and enjoys good relations with its neighbors.
    C. It has a reliable and well-developed infrastructure and an economy that is service-based.
    D. It has a unitary model of national organization and relies upon a strong military force to support the government's policies.
    E. It has its total territory divided into many governmental units and an administrative system set up to implement the policies of the central government.

Note: Examine this chart to answer question 23.

Major Exports of Selected Countries

Country A	Country B	Country C
oil	cars	computers
natural gas	televisions	airplanes
coconuts	cameras	wheat

23. Which country most accurately represents the export pattern in Column C?
    A. United States
    B. Sweden
    C. Singapore
    D. Japan
    E. Australia

24. Which of these descriptors best identifies the concept of culture as applied by human geographers?
    A. a civilized pattern of behavior
    B. an expression of artistic qualities found in music, drama, and dance
    C. a combination of habits relating to such qualities as personal hygiene and eating habits
    D. learned patterns of behavior common to a group of people
    E. habits of mind learned through formal schooling

25. One of the reasons for Japan's great industrial achievement is that as the country began to modernize, the Japanese followed a policy that
    A. opened their country to European immigration.
    B. exploited the rich resource base their country possesses.
    C. imitated many of the industrial techniques of developed nations.
    D. embarked upon a policy of colonization in the sparsely settled islands of the Pacific.
    E. encouraged proselytizing by Christian missionaries.

Free-Response Questions

Directions: As a practice exercise, students should develop answers to these two free-response questions. Both are presented as case studies and require problem solving. Responses should reflect a clear understanding of what each question expects of the student.

The Roman numerals in **bold** type accompanying each question identify the topic on the course outline which the question addresses.

1. A highly successful development company is planning to purchase a strip of land along the coast of North Carolina to build a resort community for vacationers and retirees. One of the most attractive features of the site is a fairly well preserved tidal marsh. The company's engineers have conducted several feasibility studies over the last year to determine how to use the property in a profitable yet responsible way. Of the human activities listed here, select the one that is likely to have the least negative impact on the ecosystem of the tidal marsh. Explain the rationale for your choice

      A. draining a part of the marsh to build a marina for pleasure boats

      B. constructing a pontoon bridge across the marsh with several landfill parking lots and access roads along the way for summer tourists who will visit the marsh using skimmer boats operated by the development company

      C. planning to make the marsh into a fish and game preserve for seasonal hunters and year-round fishermen

      D. donating several thousand acres of the marsh to the National Park Service to become a part of its national seashore conservation project and developing the rest as a high-rise condominium community for retirees   **I, II, and IV**

2. You live in a Maine resort town in an inlet on the ocean. A few years ago, the town council contracted to build an aquarium and develop a marina in the harbor for pleasure boats. It has been very successful attracting far more tourists than predicted. The local merchants and the marina operators welcome the new additions because both have created jobs and profits. However, other local people whose livelihood is fishing, complain that they cannot meet their catch quotas because the harbor waters where they previously dug for clams, oysters, and other mussels has shrunk. It is also dangerously polluted from over use.

As an environmentalist and a cultural geographer sensitive to the special character of coastal New England towns, you have been hired to study the situation and recommend a solution to the problem. After several months of research involving hundreds of hours of field study, you prepare to write your report. It begins with this sentence: "While the resources in this community are limited, a compromise between those promoting tourism and those anxious to protect the local fishing industry is possible."

Discuss the solution you propose to resolve this conflict about human needs and wants among the two competing groups in the town   **III and V**

•••••••••

Answer Sheet for Pre-Test in Human Geography

Multiple Choice Questions: Each answer is followed by the primary topic title from the outline of the Advanced Placement Human Geography program plus citations from *Human Geography: Culture, Society, and Space* (Sixth Edition). Students can refer to these pages for information explaining and clarifying the correct item choice. Refer to R-page citations in the reference sections of the text.

1. B Topic VII   Urbanization. (77-8, 81, 100-4)
2. E Topic VII   Urbanization. (22, 82-3, 251-2)
3. B Topic VI   Industrialization and Economic Development. (358)
4. D Topic VI   Industrialization and Economic Development. (41-map)
5. C Topic II   Population. (83-4, 95-6)

6. D Topic V   Agriculture and Rural Land Use. (219, 220, 396, R-19)
7. A Topic I   Geography: Its Nature and Perspectives. (10-1, map, R-24, R-25)
8. D Topic III   Cultural Systems and Change. (21-3, 162-3, R-24)
9. C Topic III   Cultural Systems and Change. (84, R-20)
10. E Topic VI   Industrialization and Economic Development. (285-7, 290)
11. B Topic I   Geography: Its Nature and Perspectives. (R-8, R-9)
12. E Topic III   Cultural Systems and Change. (136-7)
13. D Topic III   Cultural Systems and Change. (19, R-17)
14. B Topic VI   Industrialization and Economic Development. (289-90)
15. C Topic V   Agriculture and Rural Land Use. (197-8)
16. E Topic VII   Urbanization. (245-6)
17. A Topic IV   The Political Organization of Space. (257, 270-2)
18. B Topic IV   The Political Organization of Space. (252-4)
19. C Topic VII   Urbanization. (240-1, 251-2)
20. D Topic II   Population. (77-8)
21. C Topic II   Population. (77-8, R-47)
22. A Topic IV   The Political Organization of Space. (356, 358-9)
23. A   Topic VI   Industrial and Economic Development. (286-7)
24. D Topic IV   The Political Organization of Space. (289-91, 312)

Free-Response Questions. In answering these two questions, it is important to respond to the operative verb. In the first question, it is "explain" and in the second, it is "discuss."

1. In this question, students must first identify the option they select and then make clear the reasons for their choice. This involves presenting and developing them in detail. The three key elements that must be addressed are the nature of ecosystems and the need for environmental responsibility, the economic dimensions of the choice students make, and how human decisions and the use of the environment interact. The response will be most meaningful and persuasive when put in the context of cultural ecology (29). For background information in the text, use Part Seven on "The Geography of Modern Economic Change" and R-16, R-17, and R-18 in the glossary.

Key words to include in the answer:
    cultural ecology   development   ecosystem
    environment   human/environmental interaction
    human geography   models   region

2. In this question, student responses should examine the two positions and present both sides of the issue in a fair and objective manner. Such a presentation serves as background to the solution students must propose. That solution must be stated succinctly and forthrightly. The most likely solution is one promoting planned development and a local regulatory commission. Chapter 6 in *Human Geography in Action* will serve as a helpful resource in providing some models for dealing with the issues of employment, specialization and economic development. Because the impact of tourism is a key factor in addressing this problem, students will want to refer to the text for two excellent essays on the topic (269 and 320).

Key words to include in the answer:
    comparative advantage   tourism   planned development
    regulation   ecology   location
    spatial perspective

Chapter 5

Advanced Placement Topic I

Geography: Its Nature and Perspectives

Note: Questions on this topic will comprise five to ten percent of the Advanced Placement examination.

A. The Topic in Context - An Introduction

As the study of Earth as the home of the human family, geography examines places from a spatial and ecological perspective. To do that, it is necessary to use a variety of tools because the discipline is so complex. It bridges many areas of inquiry and in the process, reveals the relationships that exist between and among them. Napoleon's ill-fated invasion of Russia in 1812, for example, was as much a geographic event as it was an historic one - perhaps even more so. Distance, weather, and over-extended supply lines were as much his enemy as the punishing pursuit of the Russian army after the French general was forced to leave Moscow in the dead of winter. Hunger, disease, and the bitter cold forced Napoleon to abandon the campaign. His retreat across the seemingly trackless Northern European Plain was far more devastating than the enemy's guns. When he returned to Paris in the spring, his army of half a million soldiers had dwindled to a rag-tag lot of fewer than 30,000.

What Napoleon needed was a persuasive geographer with detailed maps, weather data, and an understanding of the distances separating Paris from Moscow. By dismissing scale, the vastness of the European Plain, its weather patterns, the obstacles of the region's physical features, and all other spatial associations, Napoleon ignored the processes of the physical world and allowed ambition to blind him to the geographic realities he and his army faced. More than any other factor, it was geography that shaped his destiny. Ultimately, it made his final defeat at Waterloo in June, 1815 inevitable.

If Napoleon had lived at the end of the nineteenth century rather than at its beginning, he would have had the benefit of three geographic theoreticians (Friedrich Ratzel, Sir Halford Mackinder, and Nicholas Spykman) who hypothesized about the relationship between location of a nation in Eurasia and political dominance. The speculations of these scholars typify the work of human geographers in suggesting general principles governing locational behavior and processes. When geographers embark upon such speculation, they often create models to replicate and explain reality. Even though such models are idealized representations of human phenomena, nonetheless they offer a means of focusing on issues affecting events and decisions in the real world. If Napoleon, then, had a geopolitical model to inform his judgment, perhaps he would have sought conquests along the Black Sea rather than along the Baltic.

The purpose of this topic in the Advanced Placement course is to encourage students to think geographically: to recognize that to make sense of Earth's complexity, geographers organize the world into spatial regions; to understand that geography has a special vocabulary which finds graphic representation on maps, in data bases, in photographs, pictures and other illustrations, and through field observation; and finally, to begin to use the habits of mind that distinguish geography from other systems of inquiry to define and interpret the world. The topic outline is an introduction to human geography and identifies what lies ahead in the course of study.

B. Focus Question to Direct Topic I Inquiry

When students have concluded their study of this topic, they should be able to prepare a comprehensive answer to this question:

Explain how a human geographer interprets the spatial and ecological perspectives of Earth using maps and other geographic representations, tools, and technologies in order to acquire, process and report information about peoples and their cultures.

C. Key Words/Definitions

Students should be able to define these terms and use each in such a way that its meaning is clear in the context of a sentence. Example:

Definition - Mental map: an image an individual has of an area as determined by perception, impression and knowledge; also known as a cognitive map.

Context sentence - As people become more familiar with places through study or field visits, their mental maps become increasing more accurate and precise.

Note: The citations within the parentheses next to each term identify the page numbers where it is defined and/or discussed in *Human Geography: Culture, Society, and Space*. Many terms are also included in the Glossary in Resource C (R-15-R-20).

distribution (4)
field study (2, model on introductory page of each chapter)
map (3, 5-6)
mental map (14)
model (R-21)
pattern (3)
perception (27-31)
perspective (ecological, spatial) (3-5, 7-9)
place (6)
region (formal, functional, perceptual) (13-14)
scale (7)
site (R-24)
situation (R-24)
system (R-25)
themes (6-7)
toponymy (144-46)
traditions (5-6)

D. Detailed Topic Outline/Text Correlation

Note: The citations within the parentheses identify the page numbers where information within the outline can be located in *Human Geography: Culture, Society, and Space* (Sixth Edition).

I. Topic - Geography: Its Nature and Perspective

A. Geography as a field of inquiry (3-7 with special attention to geography's five organizing themes and four traditions)

28

B. Evolution of key geographic concepts and models associated with notable geographers (Note: Students should be able to identify the following geographers, briefly explain the theory each developed, and indicate why the theory/model is important for human geographers. Preparing a chart using the references cited here will serve as a "handy go-to" document when specific geographers and their theoretical models are noted in class lectures and discussions as well as in other topics in the course of study.)

John Borchert, 255-56; Lester Brown, 200-1, 387, 392; Ernest Burgess, 261; Judith Carney, 219; Manuel Castells, 330; Walter Christaller, 258-60; Aharon Dogopolsky, 128; Clifford Geetz, 19; Peter Hall, 330; Chauncey Harris, 257, 261; Richard Hartshorne, 350; David Harvey, 332; M. J. Herskovits, 18; E. Adamson Hoebel, 18-19; Homer Hoyt, 261; Ellsworth Huntington, 30; Mark Jefferson, 235; William Jones, 123-24; August Lösch, 296; Thomas Malthus, 269; T. G. McGee, 276; Richard O'Brien, 334; William D. Pattison, 5; Friedrich Ratzel, 364; Colin Refrew, 128-29; Robert Sack, 339; Carl Sauer, 22, 25, 40, 263; August Schleicher, 124; Ruth Leger Sivard, 437, 443; Gideon Sjoberg, 234-35; John Snow, 412; Nicholas Spykman, 366; Johann Heinrich von Thünen, 200, 296; Immanuel Wallerstein, 285-86; Alfred Weber, 296; Alfred Wegener, 4.

C. Key concepts underlying the geographic perspective: *space, place, scale, change, perception, region, spatial association, pattern, process, relationship* (Note: Chapter 1 provides an excellent introduction to the concepts and perspectives identified in this section. The glossary on R-15 to R-26 provides definitions for most of these terms as well. Students should also look up the meaning of "systems" since it is an integral concept to understanding both human and physical geography.)

D. Key geographical skills
    1. How to use and think about maps and spatial data sets (7-9)
    2. How to understand and interpret the implications of associations among phenomena in places (7,9, and Toponymy, 144-46)
    3. How to recognize and interpret at different scales the relationships among patterns and processes (3,7)
    4. How to define regions and evaluate the regionalization process (6, 13, 14, 28-29)
    5. How to characterize and analyze changing interconnections among places (Language and Trade, 136-37, Patterns on the Map, 286-87)

E. Identifying sources of geographic ideas and data: field study, observation, and analysis (Note: The authors of the text have provided several helpful features illustrating the practical applications for using geographic sources, acquiring geographic data, and doing field study using observation and analysis. Students should pay special attention to these features that are common to every chapter: *At Issue, From the Field Notes, Focus On, and Applying Geographic Knowledge*).

E. Topic I Study Questions - Geography: Its Nature and Perspectives

Note: These questions will help guide the student's study of Topic I as well as serve as a review to assure knowledge and understanding of its content.

1. What are basic concepts human geographers use to study people and their cultures?
2. What is a system? Distinguish between a human and a physical system.
3. Explain why maps are considered "the language of geography." List some of the many ways they are used.
4. What is a mental or a cognitive map? Why are they important? How are they developed and improved?

5. Why are theoretical models important to human geographers? How do they relate to real-life situations?

6. Define a region. What types of regions are there? Give an example of each.

7. Explain these two analogs.
    A. Place is to geography what time is to history.
    B. A region is to a geographer what a personality type is to a psychiatrist or an era to an historian.

8. Why are maps, charts, tables, pictures and other graphics so important in the study of geography?

9. How are field studies used as tools for geographic inquiry and investigation?

10. What is toponymy? Explain why understanding toponymy reveals a great deal about what people do and value in a particular place and location.

F. Researching Topic 1 - Geography: Its Nature and Perspectives

Students will find that preparing short research papers (i.e., up to five pages) as part of the study of a topic is an effective means of deepening their understanding of its meaning and purpose within the realm of human geography. Such research serves not only as an introduction to the resources available about the topic but also as a strategy for applying the skills of organization and presentation essential to responding to the extended answer questions on the Advanced Placement examination in Human Geography.

The topics listed below serve as suggestions for the kind of research and investigation students can undertake. Each research paper should be written from an outline developed from the student's research with a brief introduction stating the hypothesis (i.e., a tentative explanation of facts tested by the investigation in the paper). A hypothesis, then, is merely a theory or a speculation that the researcher sets out to prove or disprove.

If, for example, a student wants to inquire into some aspect of toponymy (D. 2 in the Topic I outline), an appropriate hypothesis might be: Local place names are an important part of any cultural landscape. In the introduction, the hypothesis will be examined in the frame of reference of toponymy: what it is, and why and how it is important to human geographers. Including some specific illustrations (e.g., historical or religious examples such as Constantinople having a name change to Istanbul, or what place names like Corpus Christi and Santa Cruz infer about the beliefs of the of the first settlers) will add interest value as well as clarify the purpose of the hypothesis.

The body of the research paper provides the detail addressing the hypothesis. It provides precise information derived from the research the student has done and also follows the outline that has been prepared. As a result, the arguments should be well organized and logically presented. Including anecdotes and examples will make the paper more convincing and also more persuasive.

The final part of the research paper is the conclusion. That is the section providing a summary of what the student has argued and joins those arguments to the hypothesis. The purpose of the conclusion is to demonstrate why the hypothesis works (or does not work). It is the part of the paper where the writer rests the case.

To be convincing, research papers should contain citations and bibliographies. That gives them credibility. Such references also help validate the arguments the student presents. Because there is no *one* correct way to document research these days, teachers will provide the necessary guidance and direction for students relative to format. There are several widely used style manuals available. However, the three most often used to guide reporting research in human geography include:

American Psychological Association. *Publication Manual of the American Psychological Association*. 4th ed. Washington, D. C.: American Psychological Association. 1994.

Gibaldi, Joseph *MLA Handbook for Writers of Research Papers*. 4th ed. New York: Modern Language Association. 1995.

The Chicago Manual of Style. 14th ed. Chicago: University of Chicago Press. 1993.

Some Suggested Research Topics for Geography: Its Nature and Perspectives

Maps as the Language of Geography
Using Theoretical Models in Human Geography
Who Invented Geography?
Geography's Four Traditions: A Study in Perspective
Why Regionalize the World?
The Value of Field Observation in Geography
The Use of Geographic Data Bases in the Information Age
Defining Human Geography
How One Geographer Made a Difference (A case study on one of the geographers cited in part B of the outline for Topic I)
Applying the Spatial Perspective in Human Geography

G. Connecting to *Human Geography in Action*

Chapter 1 (1-1 to 1-23 plus the CD) serves as a solid introduction to human geography and reinforces many of the inclusions in the outline for Topic 1. The chapter is especially helpful in presenting different types of maps and showing students their uses and value. The CD encourages students to manipulate data on thematic maps, interpret new configurations, and draw fresh inferences. The exercises are practical and show the applications of geography to real world situations.

H. Sample Multiple-Choice Questions

These questions are typical of the kinds of questions students can expect on the examination in Advanced Placement Human Geography. Reviewing the section on multiple-choice questions in Chapter 3 of the **Study Guide** will help students better orient themselves for selecting the appropriate answer in the sample questions included here.

Directions: Each of the questions or incomplete statements is followed by five suggested answers or completions. Select the one that is best in each case.

1. The members of the city council of a mid-sized United States city have recently contracted with a team of geographers specializing in locational analysis to do a site study for a proposed regional airport. The council wants some recommendations about a site they have selected for a new airport. One of the problems the team might have in examining a series of aerial photos of the proposed site is
     A. there is too little detail showing land use activities.
     B. scale is difficult to determine.
     C. the details of relief are missing.
     D. the distribution of vegetation is obscure and imprecise.
     E. the volume of detail disguises the purpose of the map.

2. Transplanting rice as a labor intensive activity done by hand in Sichuan Province in the People's Republic of China best represents the
   A. theme of absolute location.
   B. the application of Pattison's culture-environmental tradition.
   C. similarities among the world's agricultural regions.
   D. method of rice production used universally.
   E. relationship between humans and their physical environment.

3. Which of geography's five organizing themes examines the arrangement of road networks?
   A. location
   B. place
   C. human/environmental interaction
   D. movement
   E. region

4. A researcher for a non-governmental relief agency is developing a data base on the human geography of equatorial Africa. What is an example of a correct column label that he should include on the chart?
   A. Gross Domestic Product Per Capita
   B. Key Categories of Vegetation
   C. Annual Precipitation Totals
   D. Major Landforms
   E. Acreage of National Parks/Game Preserves

5. Which one of these terms does a geographer use to identify such human phenomena as roads, ports, and rail systems?
   A. infrastructure
   B. functional specialization
   C. centripetal forces
   D. mercantilism
   E. theoretical models

6. Which of these descriptors best identifies the concept of culture as applied by human geographers?
   A. a civilized pattern of behavior
   B. an expression of artistic qualities found in music, drama, and dance
   C. a combination of habits relating to such qualities as personal hygiene and eating habits
   D. learned patterns of behavior common to a group of people
   E. the oral tradition on which a society's customs are based

7. What does a large scale map show?
   A. a large area
   B. an unbalanced area
   C. a small area
   D. an undefined area
   E. an uninhabited area

8. When geographers examine a map to determine the way places and other phenomena are presented on the cultural landscape, they are using a
     A. pattern analysis.
     B. spatial perspective.
     C. distribution measurement.
     D. scale measurement.
     E. diffusion model.

9. The map on 12 (Figure 1-6) in the text is an example of a
     A. thematic map.
     B. equal frequency map.
     C. an isoline map.
     D. a comparative analysis map.
     E. choropleth map.

10. Which of these is an example of a perceptual region?
     A. Northeast Corridor
     B. Corn Belt
     C. Central Division of the National Football League
     D. Metropolitan Tokyo
     E. Dixie

Answers: 1) C 2) E 3) D 4) A 5) A 6) D 7) C 8) B 9) A 10) E

I. Sample Free-Response Questions

These questions are similar to the free-response items likely to be on the Advanced Placement Human Geography examination.

1. Explain why theoretical models are helpful tools for human geographers in the studies they make of cultural phenomena. Provide two examples as illustrations.

2. Define spatial and cultural perspectives and compare the two to show how they are essential to the work of human geographers.

3. Explain why geographers divide the world into regions. Include illustrations describing at least two types of regions.

4. Discuss the importance of geography as a visual discipline where maps and other graphics are used to interpret the complexity of Earth.

5. The authors of the text observe in the introductory chapter: " People's perceptions of places and regions are influenced by their individual mental maps as well as by printed maps." Evaluate this statement in terms of what it suggests about the influence of culture and the importance of place.

Chapter 8

Advanced Placement Topic IV

Political Organization of Space

Note: Questions on this topic comprise thirteen to seventeen percent of the Advanced Placement examination.

A. The Topic in Context: An Introduction

Like it or not, politics is one of the realities of modern life. Not only is it an expression of a philosophy of government about how to conduct public business, but it also helps define the boundaries of places within which people live. In fact, that has been the case since the times of the earliest hunting and gathering societies. With the same authority and insistence that contemporary sovereign states exhaustively partition their territory, those ancient groups were just as manipulative. They staked their claims on regions where they could take game, catch fish, dig for roots, and harvest fruits and nuts. Only the scale and complexity of the extent of the two groups' ambitions differ. Past or present, the lesson is that territory and its governance is the power source of politics.

Through whatever governments they establish to exercise such power, people partition space for a variety of reasons. Some are motivated to create culture enclaves recognizing a common history, language, religion, and set of economic priorities; some to establish control advancing a particular social or political ideology; some to preserve an ethnic or racial identity; some to acquire more and more land area for the resources and trade opportunity it offers; and still others to increase their prestige and dominance through the development of colonies. Understandably, these efforts to divide Earth into political segments over which governments have authority are the source both cooperation and conflict. That means the relationship between and among nations is sometimes serene, sometimes strained, sometimes disruptive, but always fragile. Thus Earth's surface is ever being divided, unified, organized, and reorganized through negotiation, war, cession, and purchase.

Enter political geography. Its purpose is to explain the processes of change resulting from the constantly evolving relationships among the world's nations. It explains what boundaries exist, where they are, the policies governments develop defining their relationships with other powers, and the alliance systems they develop to promote and protect their own interests.

But as important as international relations are, political geographers recognize that political activities on a local scale have a special importance as well. Fierce debates often develop over the interpretation of census data used to delineate ward boundaries in cities and towns or the size and shape of representative districts within a state, province, or prefecture. Such arguments are almost always partisan and almost always result in gerrymandered configurations that reflect the give and take of compromise. The shape of such local entities like the shape of nation-states themselves may reflect the ability of governmental units to manage and consolidate territory. Even though a circle would be the most efficient political shape, such a compact territorial expression is as unrealistic as it is impossible, especially since the distribution of topographic features may produce physical barriers that limit the ability to govern. What remains, then, is a collection of imperfect political units - some large, some small, some symmetrical, some misshapen - that constitute the organizing territorial principal of human activities.

In the modern world where societies are increasingly technologically oriented and economies centered on service industries, the older notions of political geography as the study of a collection of sovereign units is in transformation. Today political geographers study not only local, regional, and national spatial arrangements, but also international and supranational alliance systems. These new organizational models transcend the nation-state system that has traditionally defined the world order since the end of the Middle Ages. In the current web of complex economic, military, and cultural relationships that characterize how nations presently interact, the old framework is often inadequate in dealing with the issues and problems that involve countries across the regions of the world. The extraction, distribution and pricing of petroleum is a convincing illustration of the necessity of alliance networks ensuring the availability to oil and oil products where they are needed across the globe at competitive but affordable prices.

Understanding political geography helps make sense of the interlocking systems that join, divide, and section Earth's space. Indeed political geography influences every dimension of people's lives from voting patterns and travel preferences to trade options and the consumption of goods and the use of services. Political units and the boundaries that define them constitute the divisions of the world that are locally managed and controlled but globally interconnected and interdependent.

B. Focus Question to Direct Topic IV Inquiry

When students have concluded the study of this topic, they should be able to prepare a comprehensive answer to this question:

Discuss how the forces of cooperation and conflict among the world's political units influence the division and control of Earth's surface.

C. Key Words/Definitions

Students should be able to define these terms and use each in such a way that its meaning is clear in the context of a sentence. Example:

Definition - Balkanization: the process by which a region is fragmented into smaller states which are generally hostile political units.

Context Sentence - After the breakup of the Soviet Union in 1991-92, the balkanization of some of the former republics - especially in the Caucuses region - was so destructive to internal harmony that it brought them to the brink economic collapse.

Note: The citations within the parentheses next to each term identify the pages where it is defined and/or discussed in *Human Geography: Culture, Society, and Space* (Sixth Edition). Many terms are also included in the Glossary in Resource C (R-15-R-20).

alliance system (Chapter 27 on multinationalism, 369-82)
balkanization (492-98)
boundaries (348-54)
centrifugal forces (361)
centripetal forces (359-61)
colonialism (363-65)
compact state (347)
demarcation (349)
devolution (492-98)

D. Detailed Topic Outline/Text Correlation

Note: The citations within the parentheses identify where information within the outline can be located in *Human Geography: Culture, Society, and Space* (Sixth Edition).

Topic IV - Political organization of Space

A. Nature and significance of political boundaries
    1. Ways of conceptualizing territory: from local to global (346-48)
    2. Influence of boundaries on group identity and political representation (348-54)

B. Evolution of the contemporary political pattern
    1. Territorial assumptions underlying the nation-state ideal (R-22, 341-46)
    2. Colonialism and imperialism (363-65.) While there is no single section discussing imperialism in the text, there is a good contextual discussion that explores its ramifications in several regions of the world through an a analysis of the boundaries between major religions. Refer to "Interfaith Boundaries" in Chapter 13, 174-79 as an illustration.
    3. Internal political boundaries and arrangements (359-61)

C. Challenges to inherited political-territorial arrangements
    1. Changing nature of sovereignty (337, 344, 492)
    2. Fragmentation, unification, alliance (Chapter 27 examines these topics in detail but in the rubric of "supranationalism", 369-82)

3. Spatial relationships between political patterns and patterns of ethnicity, economy, and environment (428, 429-32, 502-06)

E. Topic IV Study Questions - Political Organization of Space

1. What is political geography?
2. Why is the traditional notion of the nation-state concept presently in transition?
3. Define sovereignty. How is it manifest among the members of the family of nations?
4. Distinguish between the meaning of "country" and "nation-state."
5. In what sense are boundaries at the core of the inquiries conducted by political geographers? Identify types of boundaries and their function.
6. How are cooperation and conflict involved in influencing the distribution of social, political, and economic spaces on Earth at different scales?
7. What is the impact of multiple spatial divisions on peoples lives (e.g., school districts, congressional districts, suburban subdivisions, state and country boundaries, free trade zones etc.)?
8. What are some of the causes of border conflicts and internal territorial disputes? Provide some examples (either current or historical).
9. How do differing points of view play a role in disputes that develop over territory and resources?
10. How does a nation's shape affect both issues of governance and the development of its foreign policy?
11. How can developments such as new technologies and new markets act as change agents in a region?
12. How have colonialism and imperialism been both constructive and disruptive forces in the era since the Age of European Exploration in the sixteenth and seventeenth centuries?
13. How can efforts at religious conversion through missionary activities cause political and cultural conflict in an area?. How does it relate to the changing nature of sovereignty?
14. What are some of the forms that supranationalism takes in the contemporary world?

F. Researching Topic IV - Political Organization of Space

Students will find that preparing short research papers (i.e., up to five pages) as part of the study of a topic is an effective means of deepening their understanding of its meaning and purpose within the realm of human geography. Such research serves not only as an introduction to the resources available about the topic but also as a strategy for applying the skills of organization and presentation essential to responding to the extended answer questions on the Advanced Placement examination in Human Geography.

The topics listed below serve as suggestions for the kind of research and investigation students can undertake. Each research paper should be written from an outline developed from the student's research with a brief introduction stating the hypothesis (i.e., a tentative explanation of facts tested by the investigation in the paper). A hypothesis, then, is merely a theory or a speculation that the researcher sets out to prove or disprove.

The body of the research paper provides the detail addressing the hypothesis. It presents precise information derived from the research the student has done and also follows the outline that has been prepared. As a result, the arguments should be well organized and logically presented. Including anecdotes and examples will make the paper more convincing and also more persuasive.

The final part of the research paper is the conclusion. That is the section providing a summary of what the student has argued and joins those arguments to the hypothesis. The purpose of the conclusion is to demonstrate why the hypothesis works (or does not work). It is the part of the paper where the writer rests the case.

To be convincing, research papers should contain citations and bibliographies. That gives them credibility. Such references also help validate the arguments the student presents. Because there is no *one* correct way to document research these days, teachers will provide the necessary guidance and direction for students relative to format. There are several widely used style manuals available. However, the three most often used to guide reporting research in human geography include:

American Psychological Association. *Publication Manual of the American Psychological Association*. 4th ed. Washington, D. C.: American Psychological Association. 1994.

Gibaldi, Joseph *MLA Handbook for Writers of Research Papers*. 4th ed. New York: Modern Language Association. 1995.

The Chicago Manual of Style. 14th ed. Chicago: University of Chicago Press. 1993.

Some Suggested Research Topics for the Political Organization of Space

The Idea of the Nation
Heartland v. Rimland: Are They Theories in Conflict?
The Shapes of Countries: Do They Make a Difference?
Political Insulation: North Korea as a Case Study
Making Frontiers into Boundaries: Some Historical Examples
Geopolitics: Myth or Reality?
World Order as a Political Concept: Designing a Definition
Colonialism and the Process of Enculturation
Balancing Power: The States and the Federal Government - The American Experience
The European Union: A Case Study in Supranationalism

G. Connecting to *Human Geography in Action*

Chapter 12 on "The Rise of Nationalism and the Fall of Yugoslavia" offers a compelling case study illustrating the role political geography plays in the realignment of boundaries. Many of the concepts presented in the topic outline for this unit of study are applied in the reconfiguring of the former Yugoslavia. Map and data analysis are important components of the chapter and challenge students to "unlearn" the definitions of many political terms that are being changed and reinterpreted due to events in the international community since the end of the Cold War in 1991.

H. Sample Multiple-Choice Questions

These questions are typical of the kinds of questions students can expect on the examination in Advanced Placement Human Geography. Reviewing the section on multiple-choice questions in Chapter 3 will help students better orient themselves for selecting the appropriate answer in the sample questions included here.

Directions: Each of the questions or incomplete statements is followed by five suggested answers or completions. Select the one that is best in each case.

1. Which of the following is an example of a physical-political international boundary?
    A. railroad
    B. river
    C. canal
    D. meridian
    E. rainforest

2. All of the following are terms that connote the concept of a nation-state except
    A. linguistic.
    B. religious.
    C. ethnic.
    D. racial.
    E. political.

3. Use your mental map to classify the boundaries that define Colorado.
    A. superimposed
    B. antecedent
    C. cultural-political
    D. geometric
    E. relict

4. Why are capital cities of interest to political geographers?
    A. They are core areas always centrally located in the heart of a state.
    B. They are forward cities designed to promote their countries' political and economic objectives.
    C. Typically capital cities symbolize the cultural and historic identity of their countries.
    D. They are primarily centers of government power without any other urban functions.
    E. They are unstable governmental units that are constantly being moved to serve some special political objective.

5. Which of the following is an example of a centripetal force designed to promote national unity?
    A. an interstate highway system constructed as a military road network
    B. an educational program promoted by an ethnic group establishing its cultural dominance in a region
    C. a plan to establish a national language in a multicultural society
    D. a relocation policy to move recent immigrants to a country's underdeveloped physical regions
    E. a wall built around the capital city of a country to set it apart as a special place

6. Which statement best describes Mackinder's Heartland Theory?
    A. It proposed land-based power rather than ocean dominance as the determining factor in ruling the world.
    B. It established that a multipolar world will ensure shared power among nations.
    C. It hypothesized that because centripetal forces seldom counterbalance centrifugal forces, conflict within the international community is a constant reality.
    D. It concluded that a pivot area in the center of a landmass will always be the key factor in making a nation globally dominant.
    E. It argued that regardless of a nation's location, power would always be determined by the abundance of its natural resources.

7. Supranational organizations have become a contemporary reality largely because
    A. the state system is an inadequate instrument for dealing with world issues and problems.
    B. the collapse of the Soviet Union and the end of the Cold War has increased polarization among nation-states.
    C. nations must act unilaterally if they are to achieve their goals.
    D. nations in the developed realm need a power base to check the ambitions of nations in the developing realm.
    E. a world government is essential if there is to be international peace.

8. Political geographers argue that progress toward a unified Europe depends on
    A. agreements on refugee and displaced persons questions.
    B. the elimination of current national boundaries.
    C. a system of military alliances.
    D. the establishment of a common and stable currency.
    E. a modernized transportation network unifying the region.

9. What best characterizes the purpose of the North Atlantic Treaty Organization (NATO)?
    A. a military alliance
    B. an international peace organization
    C. an international court
    D. a nonpartisan political organization
    E. a regional economic union

10. When a country succumbs to devolutionary forces, it
    A. tends to grow stronger and more unified.
    B. develops a rapidly expanding economy.
    C. suffers a significant reduction in its population.
    D. divides along regional lines.
    E. responds to the power of centripetal forces.

Answers: 1) B 2) E 3) D 4) C 5) A 6) D 7) A 8) D 9) A 10) D

I. Sample Free-Response Questions

These questions are similar to the free-response items likely to be on the Advanced Placement Human Geography examination.

1. Contrast the unitary state model with the federal model. Identify the unifying and divisive forces of each.

2. Discuss the genetic boundary classification pioneered by Richard Hartshorne.

3. Explain why supranational alliances exist in the modern world. Provide some examples illustrating the point of the answer.

4. Assess the importance of centripetal forces as factors in unifying a political unit

5. Describe the devolutionary process and explain how it has affected particular European countries.

Chapter 9

Advanced Placement Topic V

Agricultural and Rural Land Use

Note: Questions on this topic will comprise thirteen to seventeen percent of the Advanced Placement examination.

A. The Topic in Context - An Introduction

Deep in the preliterate world of hunting and gathering, some group in some unidentified place learned - probably quite by accident - the miracle of agriculture. Its members discovered that by the deliberate tending of crops and livestock, they could provide a far more reliable food supply than what tracking wild animals, grubbing for fruits and berries, and digging for roots had to offer.

But the discovery was not confined to a single place. Rather, agriculture emerged sequentially in several regions of the world, all of which were defined by fertile soil, a moderate climate, and the availability of a reliable water supply. As a result, some 12,000 years ago, a pattern of farming activity had developed in the river valleys of the Nile, the Tigris and Euphrates, the Indus, and the Yellow (Huang He) in eastern China. The age of food producers had begun. What resulted were permanent settlements, significant population increases, the invention of written languages, and complex government structures built on an extensive system of divisions of labor.

More than any other human activity, agriculture changed Earth's cultural landscape in ways that have not only transformed the way people live but also make it possible for billions of them to successfully inhabit today's world. Unlike other transformations, however, agriculture developed in several stages. Historians and human geographers call these *revolutions* because they wrought changes that have had a deep and enduring impact on both life styles and settlement patterns. To date, there have been three of these revolutions, each dramatic but shaping, and each complicated but consequential. The first achieved plant and animal domestication, a global process that took thousand of years to accomplish; the second, centered in Europe during the Middle Ages and prelude to the Industrial Revolution, involved improved methods of cultivating, producing and storing food; and the third called the Green Revolution is still in progress. Using sophisticated technology and research into the genetic make-up of food commodities, this revolution has increased crop yields to support the demands of a soaring world population. Without the success of this revolution, global famine would be as much a reality and as devastating as both epidemics and nuclear war.

Human geographers examine agricultural and rural land use in order to understand the disparities in the world production and distribution of food. They also study the reasons for overproduction in some regions and underproduction in others. Understanding the complex environmental and technological reasons for these inequities provides a frame of reference for finding solutions to providing food supplies on a more fair basis for all the world. But certain factors are beyond their control. These involve the often perplexing patterns of trade and the uncertainty of the world's markets as well as conflicts between poor farmers with little land and rich ones with great aggregates of acreage.

Among the tools human geographers use to aid in their understanding of the positive and negative aspects of the patterns of agricultural production is the spatial model. Even though these models are idealized representations of reality, nonetheless they simplify the complex and facilitate the search for solutions. The Von Thünen's Spatial Model of Farming is an example. Even though several centuries old, it still has application, and continues to be central to the study of rural geography.

Much of Earth's surface is devoted to agricultural activity. Over the millennia, it has created cultural landscapes that have changed all the world's regions. Rolling wheat lands in North America, Australia, Argentina, and on the Ukrainian steppes to terraced hill slopes in Asia to slash and burn patches in Amozonia testify to the extent of farming. Human geography examines all the factors that continually challenge the ability of farmers to secure an adequate food supply and accommodate to the fragile balance between supply and demand on a global scale.

B. Focus Question to Direct Topic V Inquiry

When students have concluded their study of this topic, they should be able to prepare a comprehensive answer to this question:

Describe how the Von Thünen Model of Farming developed in early nineteenth century Europe helps explain rural spatial patterns common to the First and Second Agricultural Revolutions as well as to those resulting from the Third Agricultural Revolution.

C. Key Words/Definitions

Students should be able to define these terms and use each in such a way that its meaning is clear in the context of a sentence. Example:

Definition - Wattle: construction processes used in traditional buildings employing poles intertwined tightly with twigs, reeds, or branches, and then plastered with mud; used for walls, fences and other enclosures, and roofs

Context Sentence - Wattle buildings are common sights on the rural landscapes of Southeast Asia because of the ample availability of the materials used in the construction of such structures.

Note: The citations within the parentheses next to each term identify where it is defined and/or discussed in *Human Geography: Culture, Society, and Space.* (Sixth Edition) Many terms are also included in the Glossary in Resource C (R-15-R-20)

agribusiness (219)
agriculture (190)
Agricultural Revolutions
     • First/Neolithic (193)
     • Second (199)
     • Third (199-201, 220)
     • Green Revolution (219, 220, 387, 396)
commercial/industrial agriculture (219-20)
cultural landscape (21-23, 162-63)
diffusion (196)
     • diffusion routes (210)
     • maladaptive diffusion (210)
dispersed settlement (203)
domestication
     • animal (195-96)
     • plant (193-94)

economic activities
  • primary (189)
  • secondary (189)
  • tertiary (189-90)
extractive economic activity (189)
hamlet (210)
maladaptive diffusion (210)
nucleated/agglomerated settlement (203, 240)
paleolithic (R-22)
shifting cultivation (197)
subsistence farming (196-98)
Thünian patterns (200)
traditional architecture (209)
village (210-13)
Von Thünen's Spatial Model of Farming/Von Thünen's Model of Agricultural Location (200)

D. Detailed Topic Outline/Text Correlation

Note: The citations within the parentheses identify where information within the outline can be located in *Human Geography: Culture, Society, and Space* (Sixth edition).

Topic V. Agricultural and Rural Land Use

A. Development and diffusion of agriculture (Note Figure 16-1 on 216-17 as a reference guide showing the regionalization of the world's agriculture based on primary farming activity.)
  1. First/Neolithic Agricultural Revolution (193)
  2. Evolution of energy sources and technology ("Key Points," 189, "Classifying Economic Activities," 189-90)
  3. Regions of plant and animal domestication (190-98, Figure 14-2 on 193)

B. Major agricultural production regions
  1. Agricultural systems associated with major bio-climatic zones ("Subsistence Farming," 196-98, and Chapter 16, 214-22)
  2. Production and food supply: linkages and flows ("Diffusion," 196, 218-22)

C. Rural land use and change
  1. Location and land use models (Examine the Von Thünen Model (200) and the achievements of the three agricultural revolutions, (193, 199, 199-201, 220)
  2. Intensification and land use (Table 14-1, 194, and the discussion on "Domestication," 193-96)
  3. Settlement systems (Chapter 15, 202-13 on "Rural Settlement Forms")

D. Impacts of modern agricultural change
  1. Green Revolution (219, 220, 387, 396)
  2. Consumption, nutrition, and hunger (Chapter 28, 387-94 on "A Geography of Nutrition")
  3. Industrial/commercial agriculture (219, 220 including "The Third Agricultural Revolution")
  4. Environmental change (473-76): desertification (461-62), deforestation (462-64, 476, 478), farmland loss to urban growth (395, 398), greenhouse warming effect (45), acid rain (461)

E. Topic V Study Questions - Agricultural and Rural Land Use

1. Describe the difference between paleolithic and neolithic societies.
2. What role did fire and metallurgy play in hunting and gathering societies and in early agricultural communities?
3. Why are fishing and lumbering included in the study of agricultural geography?
4. What is the significance of the First Agricultural Revolution?
5. Describe the three levels of economic activities that show the range from simple to complex and from ancient practices to modern ones..
6. Why is agriculture classified as a part of the extractive sector in the hierarchy of economic activities?
7. What is subsistence agriculture? In what regions of today's world does it still prevail?
8. Explain the relationship between plant and animal domestication and agricultural practice.
9. Describe some of the practical alternatives to subsistence agriculture.
10. Identify the Second Agricultural Revolution. How did it differ from the First Agricultural Revolution?
11. What is the nature of the Third Agricultural Revolution (which is still in progress)? Why is it also identified as the Green Revolution?
12. Discuss Von Thünen's Model of Farming. Relate the model to soil quality and climate changes.
13. Why are human geographers interested in the nature of human settlement?
14. Distinguish between dispersed and nucleated settlements.
15. Explain how the forms, functions, materials, and spacing of rural dwellings (and settlements) reveal a great deal about a region and its culture. How are these manifestations of human/environmental interaction?
16. Describe commercial agriculture. What is the relationship between the development of commercial agriculture and European colonial policy over the last two centuries?
17. What conclusions can be drawn about the patterns of world agriculture by studying Figure 16.1 on page 216?
18. Assess the impact of changing agricultural practices in (a) North America. (b) Latin America, and (c) Africa.
19. Describe some of the risks implicit in single crop economies.
20. Explain why the global network of farm production is more responsive to the needs of the urbanized societies of the industrialized democracies in the developed world than to more marginal societies in the developing world.

F. Researching Topic V - Agricultural and Rural Land Use

Students will find that preparing short research papers (i.e., up to five pages) as part of the study of a topic is an effective means of deepening their understanding of its meaning and purpose within the realm of human geography. Such research serves not only as an introduction to the resources available about the topic but also as a strategy for applying the skills of organization and presentation essential to responding to the extended answer questions on the Advanced Placement examination in Human Geography.

The topics provided here are certainly not comprehensive and all-inclusive, but only serve as suggestions for the kind of research and investigation students can undertake. Each research paper should be written from an outline developed from the student's research with a brief introduction stating the hypothesis (i.e., a tentative explanation that accounts for a set of facts that will be tested by the investigation presented in the paper). A hypothesis, then, is merely a theory or a speculation that the researcher sets out to prove or disprove..

The body of the research paper provides the detail addressing the hypothesis. It provides precise information derived from the research the student has done and also follows the outline that has been prepared. As a result, the arguments should be well organized and logically presented. Including anecdotes and examples will make the paper more convincing and also more persuasive.

The final part of the research paper is the conclusion. That is the section providing a summary of what the student has argued and joins those arguments to the hypothesis. The purpose of the conclusion is to demonstrate why the hypothesis works (or does not work). It is the part of the paper where the writer rests the case.

To be convincing, research papers should contain citations and bibliographies. That gives them credibility and it also helps validate the arguments the student presents. Because there is no *one* correct way to document research these days, teachers will provide the necessary guidance and direction for students There are several widely used style manuals available. However, the three most often used to guide reporting research in human geography include:

American Psychological Association. *Publication Manual of the American Psychological Association*. 4th ed. Washington, D. C.: American Psychological Association. 1994.

Gibaldi, Joseph *MLA Handbook for Writers of Research Papers*. 4th ed. New York: Modern Language Association. 1995.

The Chicago Manual of Style. 14th ed. Chicago: University of Chicago Press. 1993.

Some Suggested Research Topics for Agricultural and Rural Land Use

Thomas Malthus and the Malthusian Equation: An Evaluation
The World's Principal Food Crops: Their Distributions and Their Markets
Factors Influencing Land Use: Examining Models as Production Determinants
The Green Revolution and Problems of Increasing Food Production
International Law and the Regulation of the World's Fishing Areas
In Search of New Technologies: Aquaculture and the Use of Hybrids
Barriers to Increasing Agricultural Production in the Developing World
Wheat and Rice as Cultural Indicators: A Case Study
Modernization and Changing Residential Traditions in Rural Settlements
The Three Agricultural Revolutions: A Contrast in the Study of Spatial Settings

G. Connecting to *Human Geography in Action*

Chapter 13 (13-1 to 13-24) examines the ways humans can have an impact on the environment. It connects them to the primary, secondary, and tertiary sectors of the economy as a means of providing a realistic context. The emphasis is on the positive and negative results of environmental change. Thus, students are challenged to examine the causal relationships affecting people and their environments. The chapter has a strong agricultural orientation and complements virtually every aspect of Topic V.

H.   Sample Multiple-Choice Questions

These questions are typical of the kinds of questions students can expect on the examination in Advanced Placement Human Geography. Reviewing the section on multiple-choice questions in Chapter 3 will help students better orient themselves for selecting the appropriate answer in the sample questions included here.

Directions: Each of the questions or incomplete statements is followed by five suggested answers or completions. Select the one that is best in each case.

1. What is the hypothesis relating to food production and agriculture that Thomas Malthus established in his essay on population?
   A. There are no controls available to limit population growth.
   B. Food production increases arithmetically as population increases geometrically.
   C. The positive checks on population growth are war, famine, and disease.
   D. Government policy is the only effective control on population growth.
   E. Earth's capacity to produce food consistently outruns natural increases in the population.

2. Von Thünen's spatial model of farming is predicated on what theoretical construct?
   A. concentric rings
   B. irregular distribution patterns
   C. linear distributions
   D. interrelated stages of development
   E changing residential styles

3. Which of the following is an example of a nucleated settlement pattern?
   A. Villages are located along a narrow road at approximately half mile intervals.
   B. People live in widely scattered and ill-formed settlements.
   C. Houses and other buildings are grouped in clusters.
   D. Settlements are singly on small plots where there are no dwellings or out buildings.
   E. Human activity follows a consistent but irregular distribution pattern.

4. Which of the following is illustrative of maladaptive diffusion?
   A. a teepee on the prairies of North America
   B. a yurt on the Mongolian steppe
   C. a ranch house in New Mexico
   D. a three decker apartment building in an urban neighborhood in Worcester, MA
   E. a Phoenix subdivision comprised of Cape Cod style houses

5. How do human geographers identify the smallest cluster of houses and non-residential buildings?
   A. as a village
   B. as a town
   C. as a hamlet
   D. as a cooperative
   E. as a borough

6. Identify the primary cause of the Third Agricultural Revolution.
   A. crop diversification
   B. global warming
   C. government subsidies
   D. biotechnology
   E. success at stabilizing the world's population

7. What is the general location of the largest areas of commercial farms?
   A. in tropical zones
   B. in North America
   C. in the temperate zones
   D. in the countries of the former Soviet Union
   E. in Subsaharan Africa

8. The primary reason for the increased success of agriculture on a global scale global is directly related to
    A. the decisions of the United Nations Security Council and General Assembly.
    B. the policies of the United States Department of Agriculture.
    C. the worldwide commercialization of farming.
    D. the recent advances in technology and genetic engineering.
    E. the decline in subsistence farming and slash and burn techniques.

9. The processes of shifting cultivation most directly relates to
    A. the First Agricultural Revolution.
    B. the Second Agricultural Revolution.
    C. The Green Revolution.
    D. hunting and gathering economies.
    E. subsistence farming.

10. Which of the following is an example of a tertiary economic activity?
    A. forestry, lumbering, and mining
    B. herding, hunting, and gathering
    C. manufacturing chemical fertilizers
    D. working in a service industry
    E. commercial wheat cultivation

Answers: 1) B 2) A 3) C 4) E 5) C 6) D 7) C 8) D 9) E 10) D

I. Sample Free-Response Questions

These questions are similar to the free-response items likely to be on the Advanced Placement Human Geography examination.

1. To answer this question, refer to Figure 16.1 on 216-17 in the text. Compare the climatic relationships in similar crop-growing areas around the world. Explain the reasons for the relationships you observe.

2. Explain how each of the three agricultural revolutions affected food production in their respective historical periods.

3. Describe the relationships that exist between housing styles and the physical environment. What accounts for such phenomena as maladaptive diffusion?

4. Discuss how European colonialism was responsible for permanently changing farming practices in the regions of its influence around the world.

5. Explain why rural life has been consistently dominated by primary economic activities regardless of place or time period.

Chapter 10

Advanced Placement Topic VI

Industrialization and Economic Development

Note: Questions on this topic will comprise thirteen to seventeen percent of the Advanced Placement examination.

A. The Topic in Context - An Introduction

In a world becoming increasingly more globalized, human geographers are challenged to understand and interpret economies of scale. These identify the various levels of development across the world's regions. In some areas, people live at the subsistence level as marginalized farmers on meager patches of unproductive land, but in others, they cultivate thousands of acres on commercial farms using the latest technology and applying the principles of agribusiness. In yet other places, some people prosper in cities providing services through one the professions or in managerial positions for multi-national and transnational corporations. In the same urban setting, others endure low-paying jobs requiring minimal literacy or only the most basic of skills.

Enormous gaps exist between rich and poor classes within many countries and between rich and poor countries as well. Regional disparities abound. In some places, the pace of economic change is so rapid, it is staggering. Growth is constant and powerful. In other areas, economies stagnate with millions of workers idle or only seasonally employed. Families barely exist on the fringe of survival. Life changes little. People live in abject poverty eking out minimal livings for themselves and their children often in subhuman conditions.

Economic geographers use a variety of strategies to explain why these disparities exist, why they are so extreme, why they are where they are, and how they can be eliminated - or at least narrowed. One recent approach is to analyze regional and national economies using the core-periphery model as a means of understanding the economic relationships among places. This model views the world as an integrated whole where the laws of change are anything but absolute. It recognizes that development is complex and cannot be reduced to simple categories. A variety of factors, then, determines growth or decline at both the core and the periphery.

The economic stability of the contemporary world is being shaped by industrialization. Indeed in many places, it is the only key to development, with the possible exception of tourism. Even agriculture has been either diminished as a primary activity or even totally abandoned.

For prosperity to result from industrializing, care must be given to the location of plants and factories so that they have all the elements of production assuring economic success in an increasingly specialized world (i.e., a single item's parts being made in many places and sent to a single location for assembly and transport to other places across the globe). As a result, the manufacture of goods in recent decades means that industry is presently undergoing a global shift with significant implications for the future in both the core and the periphery nations. The one factory town model, for example, that once characterized the economy of much of New England is now a relic.

Yet once industrialization has been realized, there is a another phase of economic development. It is the transition that shifts an economy from production to service and ultimately from service to the processing and analysis of information. Human geographers call these phenomena deindustrialization. What this means is that declining industrialization in the core is fundamentally altering global patterns of economic well-being largely because labor-intensive manufacturing has moved to the periphery.

The entire realm of economic geography is in transition. It is in search of new definitions and new models. The role of world cities is a case in point. These are the control centers that host the multinational and supranational cores that drive the global economy. Their role and function transcends national boundaries. What occurs in one part of the world may well be the result of a decision made in a city half a world away. In many ways, these cities are increasingly doing for finance, production, and distribution what has typically been the role of nation-states. What is emerging, then, is a new world economic order far more complex and far more difficult to understand than the former and more simple systems.

B. Focus Question to Direct Topic VI Inquiry

When students have concluded their study of this topic, they should be able to prepare a comprehensive answer to this question:

What are the forces of modern economic change that encourage some national economies to grow and flourish and others to either stagnate or decline?

C. Key Words/Definitions

Students should be able to define these terms and use each in such a way that its meaning is clear in the context of a sentence. Example:

Definition - Cartel: a combination of independent business organizations formed to regulate production, pricing, and marketing of goods by the members

Context Sentence - The Organization of Petroleum Exporting Countries (OPEC) is a cartel in which joint pricing policies are largely responsible for the cost of gas at the pump in the United States.

Note: The citations within the parentheses next to each term identify where it is defined and/or discussed in *Human Geography: Culture, Society, and, Space* (Sixth Edition). Many terms are also included in the Glossary in Resource C (R-15-R-20)

agglomeration (296)
basic/non-basic activities (R-15-16)
break-of-bulk point (R-16, 308)
cartel (R-16)
core region (R-17)
core-periphery model (R-16, 285-86)
dependency theory (R-17, 220, 290)
developed country (284-85)
developing country (284-85)
economic reach (R-18, 257)
economic tiger (R-18)
economic sector (189-90, 320)
entrepôt (R-18)
feudalism (R-18, 234)
globalization (R-19, 270, 503)
Gross National Product (GNP) (R-19, 283, 284)

industrial location theory (296)
infrastructure (R-19, 299)
least cost theory (295)
liberal models (289)
manufacturing export zones (R-21, 329)
maquiladora (R-21, 309, 326)
mercantilism (R-21, 236)
Modernization Model of Economic Development (R-21, 290)
multinationals (R-21, 375-82)
multiplier effect (R-21, 257)
natural resource (R-22)
new industrial division of labor (R-22, 322-27)
North American Free Trade Agreement (NAFTA) (R-21, 308, 381)
per capita (R-22)
peripheral region (R-22, 288-89)
postindustrial (R-23)
preindustrialism (234-36)
primary economic activity (R-23)
primary industrial region (303-04)
renewable resource (R-24)
secondary economic activity (R-23)
secondary industrial region (315-16)
semi-peripheral region (R-240)
Special Economic Zones (SEZs) (315)
structuralist model (289)
tertiary economic activity (R-25, 319)
time-space compression (324-25)
underdevelopment (284-85)
variable cost (295)
Weber's least cost theory (295-96)
world city model (290)
world systems theory "Industrial Location Theory," 296)

D. Detailed Topic Outline/Text Correlation

Note: The citations within the parentheses identify where information within the outline can be located in *Human Geography: Culture, Society, and Space* (Sixth Edition).

VI. Topic - Industrialization and Economic Development

A. Character of industrialization (Note: Students will find that "A Changing World" (290-91) provides a brief but comprehensive introduction to Topic VI by showing the relationship between politics and economics in a world community becoming increasingly more globalized.)
　　1. Economic sectors: primary, secondary, tertiary, and quatenary (189-90, 320)
　　2. Specialization in places and the concept of comparative advantage (240)
　　(Note: The concept of "comparative advantage" is not discussed by that identifier in *Human Geography: Culture, Society, and Space* (Sixth Edition). However, it is addressed in "Measures of Development" (285) and in the treatment of specialization (240). Economic geographers define "comparative advantage" as a country's ability to produce a product relatively more effectively than another because of its relative location and the resources it possesses.)
　　3. Transport and communications (285, 298)
　　4. Models of industrial location (Figure 21-1 on 286-87, 294-300)

67

B. Spatial aspects of the rise of industrial economies
    1. Changing energy sources and technology (299-300, 306, 395, 474-76)
    2. Economic cores and peripheries (285-86)
    3. Models of economic development and their geographic critiques (284, 285, 289-91)

C. Contemporary global patterns of industrialization/resource extraction (Note: Chapter 23 provides a comprehensive discussion of current trends in economic development and industrialization in key world regions.)
    1. Linkages and interdependencies (298)
    2. Changing patterns of industrial activity and deindustrialization (328-34)

D. Impacts of industrialization (Note: Chapter 32 deals with the topics in this section extensively. It examines how humans have altered the environment over the millennia and how in recent years, they have been able to affect environmental change on a global scale both positively and negatively.)
    1. Time-space compression ("Industrial Location Theory," 296)
    2. Social stratification (cf. "structuralist theory" on 290)
    3. Health, quality of life, and hazards ("Nonvectored Infectious Diseases" and "Chronic Diseases," 410-16)
    4. Environmental change and issues of sustainability (455-56)

E. Topic VI Study Questions - Industrialization and Economic Development

1. Define economic geography.
2. Compare and contrast the differences that distinguish the developing from the developed world
3. Describe some of the disparities in the core-periphery relationships among different regions of the world.
4. Discuss the relationship between politics and economic development. Use specific examples to illustrate the points you make in your essay.
5. Select one of the two models for development (i.e., liberal or structuralist) described in the chapter and analyze its strengths and weaknesses in terms of facilitating or inhibiting a country's economic growth.
6. Describe the five stages of Rostow's "modernization model." Evaluate its accuracy as a predictor of a country's struggle for economic development.
7. Describe location theory. Discuss how it helps explain the spatial positioning of industries and their success or failure.
8. Explain why there are regional economic differences within a country.
9. Describe Weber's least cost theory. Explain why it has been so hotly debated among economic geographers.
10. Describe the physical and human features commonly shared by the world's four major industrial regions (i.e., Western and Central Europe, Eastern North America, Russia-Ukraine, Eastern Asia).
11. Using a cultural and an environmental perspective, evaluate the major positive and negative impacts of industrialization.
12. Explain the causes of deindustrialization. Explain why the tertiary and quatenary economic sectors are the replacements for industrialization.
13. Evaluate the importance of the maquiladora as new economic expressions in the world economy.

F. Researching Topic VI - Industrialization and Economic Development

Students will find that preparing short research papers (i.e., up to five pages) as part of the study of a topic is an effective means of deepening their understanding of its meaning and purpose within the realm of human geography. Such research serves not only as an introduction to the resources available about the topic but also as a strategy for applying the skills of organization and presentation essential to responding to the extended answer questions on the Advanced Placement examination in Human Geography.

The topics provided here are certainly not comprehensive and all-inclusive, but only serve as suggestions for the kind of research and investigation students can undertake. Each research paper should be written from an outline developed from the student's research with a brief introduction stating the hypothesis (i.e., a tentative explanation that accounts for a set of facts that will be tested by the investigation presented in the paper). A hypothesis, then, is merely a theory or a speculation that the researcher sets out to prove or disprove.

The body of the research paper provides the detail addressing the hypothesis. It provides precise information derived from the research the student has done and also follows the outline that has been prepared. As a result, the arguments should be well organized and logically presented. Including anecdotes and examples will make the paper more convincing and also more persuasive.

The final part of the research paper is the conclusion. That is the section providing a summary of what the student has argued and joins those arguments to the hypothesis. The purpose of the conclusion is to demonstrate why the hypothesis works (or does not work). It is the part of the paper where the writer rests the case.

To be convincing, research papers should contain citations and bibliographies. That gives them credibility and it also helps validate the arguments the student presents. Because there is no *one* correct way to document research these days, teachers will provide the necessary guidance and direction for students There are several widely used style manuals available. However, the three most often used to guide reporting research in human geography include:

American Psychological Association. *Publication Manual of the American Psychological Association*. 4th ed. Washington, D. C.: American Psychological Association. 1994.

Gibaldi, Joseph *MLA Handbook for Writers of Research Papers*. 4th ed. New York: Modern Language Association. 1995.

The Chicago Manual of Style. 14th ed. Chicago: University of Chicago Press. 1993.

Some Suggested   Research Topics on Industrialization and Economic Development

Defining the Developed and the Developing World
The Gross National Product and the Quality of Life in the Developing World: Exploring A Relationship
Examining A Pre-Industrial Society: A Case Study (e.g., Niger, Mali, Burkina Faso, Somalia, etc.)
Why Some Countries Are Rich and Some Countries Are Poor: An Analysis
Alfred Weber and His Theories of Industrial Location: An Explanation
Geopolitics: An Authentic Inquiry Model or a Pseudo Science?
Tourism as an Economic Activity
Politics and Economic Development: An Essential Relationship
What Makes A Corporation Transnational?

G. Connecting to *Human Geography in Action*

Chapter 6 (6-1 to 6-22) provides some practical applications of economic geography. In addition to reinforcing information about the several levels of economic activity described in *Human Geography: Culture, Society, and Space* (Sixth Edition), it asks students to compare their state's economic profile to the national profile now and thirty years earlier. It also provides some exercises that relate to the contemporary job market showing the relationship between geography (location, site, access to transport and materials, etc.) and jobs using regional multipliers.

H. Sample Multiple-Choice Questions

These questions are typical of the kinds of questions students can expect on the examination in Advanced Placement Human Geography. Reviewing the section on multiple-choice questions in Chapter 3 will help students better orient themselves for selecting the appropriate answer in the sample questions included here.

Directions: Each of the questions or incomplete statements is followed by five suggested answers or completions.. Select the one that is best in each case.

1. Which of these factors is vital to economic development?
    A. a population with a high doubling time
    B. a country with a high Gross National Product
    C. an available and abundant natural resource
    D. a well developed transport system
    E. a high literacy rate

2. What term do economic geographers use to identify organizations promoting political, economic, and/or cultural cooperation to promote some shared objective?
    A. supranational
    B. international
    C. traditional
    D. interdependent
    E. national

3. What is the main focus of activities functioning in the tertiary sector of an economic system?
    A. automobile manufacturing
    B. agriculture
    C. acquiring and processing information
    D. hunting and fishing
    E. providing services

4. What is the function of the maquiladora in the modern-day economy?
    A. These are foreign-owned plants that assemble imported goods for export.
    B. These are factory incentive zones that have been funded in the cities of the developing world by the International Monetary Fund.
    C. These are a category of agricultural migrant workers who receive government subsidies to settle permanently in Latin America's industrial cities.
    D. These are cattle ranches in the Rio Grande Valley that grow cattle for export to the protein-deprived countries in the developing world.
    E. These are high energy consumption regions in eastern North America and Western Europe where nuclear power is the primary energy source.

5. What two features best characterize the changes affected by the Industrial Revolution?
    A. service industries and information processing
    B. technological innovation and specialization
    C. improved farm implements and the development of hybrid seeds
    D. higher literacy rates and decreased population doubling time
    E. well-equipped professional armies and the deployment of nuclear weapons

6. What element is basic to Weber's least cost theory in determining the location of an industrial site?
    A. power supplies
    B. labor costs
    C. availability of transportation
    D. proximity to markets
    E. quantity of raw materials

7. Which of these statements about core-periphery relationships is correct in characterizing the global economic system?
    A. It works to the advantage of periphery countries.
    B. It works to the disadvantage of core countries.
    C. It works to the advantage of both core and periphery countries.
    D. It works to the disadvantage of periphery countries.
    E. It is irrelevant in a complex worldwide economic system.

8. In Walt Rostow's modernization model identifying the levels and stages of economic development, in what sector of the economy are most workers employed in those few countries achieving the fifth stage?
    A. extractive
    B. service
    C. industrial
    D. professional
    E. agticultural

9. All of the following are typical criteria for determining if a country is developing and peripheral except
    A. a high birth rate.
    B. a high infant mortality rate.
    C. a high unemployment rate.
    D. a high energy consumption per capita rate.
    E. a high per capita GNP rate

10. The growth or decline of secondary industries can be influenced by factors not always accounted for by models but determined by such factors as
    A. political instability.
    B. the availability of raw materials.
    C. an adequate labor force.
    D. access to transportation.
    E. a reasonable agglomeration.

Answers: 1) E 2) A 3) E 4) A 5) B 6) C 7) D 8) B 9) D 10) A

I. Sample Free-Response Questions

These questions are similar to the free-response items likely to be on the Advanced Placement Human Geography examination.

1. Explain why there are regional economic differences within a country.

2. Select one of the development models that human geographers use to assess a country's economic progress. Evaluate its strengths and weaknesses.

3. Analyze Weber's least cost theory as it relates to the processes of Japan's industrialization resulting from the Meiji Restoration in 1867.

4. Compare the challenges of economic development in any two of the world's developing countries.

5. Provide three reasons why tourism is a mixed blessing for peripheral nations. Discuss each one as it positively and negatively affects local economies.

Chapter 11

Advanced Placement Topic VII

Cities and Urban Land Use

Note: Questions on this topic will comprise thirteen to seventeen percent of the Advanced Placement examination.

A. The Topic in Context - An Introduction

After the invention of agriculture, more densely populated settlements were its logical extension. With farms able to provide a constant and generally reliable food supply for large numbers of people, it was possible for human groups to cluster in places varying in size, composition, location, arrangement and function, and address issues beyond the basic struggle to acquire the essentials of food, clothing, and shelter. Known variously over the centuries as hamlets, villages, towns, and cities, these groupings of habitation have become the focus of most aspects of life. They are centers of social and economic activities, political and administrative systems, transportation and communication networks, and cultural and educational opportunities. As such, they exercise a powerful influence on styles of life, on the development of patterns of culture, and on the quality of contacts groups have with each other. Although settlements across the world differ markedly, nonetheless knowing their processes and functions is central to a knowledge of human geography.

Cities as the largest and densest of human settlements have become the nodes of modern society. Now almost half of the world's people live in them. Indeed in some of its industrialized regions, seventy-five percent of the population inhabits urban areas. The trend of rapid growth is a constant everywhere. Such cities as Tokyo, Cairo, and São Paulo cover vast areas where population densities number in the hundreds - even thousands - per square mile. And the phenomenon of megalopolis, a web of interconnected metropolitan areas such as the one stretching from Washington, D.C. to Boston, is an undeniable reality everywhere in the world.

But not all urban growth has been as intense as it is today. Historically, cities have evolved in stages. The fortress city of the ancient world became the administrative and trading center of later times. With the Industrial Revolution, factory-dominated manufacturing cores replaced the earlier city models which were the focus of commerce, learning, and religion. With the coming of the automobile, these factory towns gave way to the suburbanized modern cities where great tracts of land have been transformed from rural to urban uses at increasingly greater distances from the old downtowns. And now human geographers are beginning to study the emergence of the postmodern city, a product of technologically advanced societies. As an entrepreneurial and information center, its function is clear, but its form is not.

The urbanization that has become one of the connecting threads of the modern world is not problem-free. Urban influences have significantly affected human geography. Primate cities, megacities, and megalopolises exercise preeminent influences on the culture, politics, economics, and social values of their countries. Wherever their location, their problems are cross-cultural. Such problems may differ in degree but not in kind. Pollution, strained infrastructures, substandard housing, congestion, crime, and poor schools are as evident in the cities of North and South America as they are in Europe, Asia, or Africa. These conditions stand in sharp contrast to the vitality and energy also associated with modern cities. Learning to reduce these contrasts and improve the quality of urban life is the challenge all cities face.

B. Focus Question to Direct Topic VII Inquiry

When students have concluded their study of this topic, they should be able to prepare a comprehensive answer to this question:

Compare and contrast the similarities and differences among the cities of the ancient world, those of preindustrial Europe, and modern cities designed on western models.

C. Key Words/Definitions

Students should be able to define these terms and use each in such a way that its meaning is clear in the context of a sentence. Example:

Definition - <u>Urban System</u>: the functional and spatial organization of cities (e.g., transportation modes, street design and layout, the location of shopping and recreation areas, etc.)

Context Sentence - As Brasilia was being conceptualized as Brazil's capital city, planners had the opportunity to invent an entirely new <u>urban system</u>.

Note: The citations within the parentheses next to each term identify where it is defined and/or discussed in *Human Geography: Culture, Society, and Space* (Sixth Edition). Many terms are also included in the Glossary in Resource C (R-15-R-20)

agglomeration (R-15, 240, 296)
Borchert, John (255-56)
central business district (CBD) (R-16, R-24, 241, 260, 266)
central place (R-16, 257)
central place theory (R-16, 257-58)
Christaller, Walter (258-60)
cityscape (263)
concentric zone model (R-16, 261)
conurbation (R-16)
deglomeration (R-17, 267)
feudal city (R-19, 234)
gentrification (268)
hamlet (210)
hinterland (R-20, 240)
Industrial Revolution (R-20, 294)
infrastructure (R-20, 299)
inner city (266, 267-70)
megacity (243, 249-51)
megalopolis (R-21, 241, 247-49)
mercantile city (R-21, 236)
metropolis (R-25, 241)
multiple nuclei model (R-21, 261)
postmodern city (R-23)
preindustrial city (237)
primate city (R-23, 234-35)
sector model (R-24, 261)
site (R-24)
situation (R-24)
social stratification (R-24, 41)

suburb (R-24, 241, 260, 270)
urban form (262-64)
urban function (256)
urban geography (R-25, 240)
urban hierarchy (R-19, R-25, 240)
urban models (262-64)
urban morphology (R-25, 263)
urban realms (R-25, 260-62)
urban site (243-44)
urban spatial structure (256-58)
urban system (R-26)
urbanization (R-26)
village (210-13)
world city (R-26, 328-29)
zoning (251)

D. Detailed Topic Outline/Text Correlation

Note: The citations within the parentheses identify where information within the outline can be located in *Human Geography: Culture, Society, and Space* (Sixth edition).

VII. Topic - Cities and Urban Land Use

A. Definitions of Urbanism (R-26, 227)

B. Origin and evolution of cities (Chapter 17 on "Urbanization and Civilization" offers a complete discussion of this topic, 227-37)
    1. Historical patterns of urbanization (Chapter 17 provides comprehensive coverage showing the evolution of cities from ancient times to the present, 227-37.)
    2. Cultural context and urban form (Comments on agglomeration, specialization, urban geography and the ranking of urban centers are especially helpful, 240-41.)
    3. Urban growth and rural-urban migration (John Borchert's model provides an historical context on this sub-topic, 254-56)
    4. Rise of megacities (249-51)
    5. Models of urban systems (256-64. Special attention should be paid to "Focus On" on 261)
    6. Comparative models of internal city structure (The essay on "Models of Urban Structure" in Chapter 19, 260-264, describes the differences in the form of cities in various parts of the world. Chapter 20 on "Changing Cities in a Changing World" also examines the structure of cities around the world and discusses the impact of globalization on them as well as the emergence of world cities in the late twentieth century, 266-77.)

C. Functional character of contemporary cities (Chapter 20, 266-77)
    1. Changing employment mix (256-58)
    2. Changing demographic and social structures ("A Sense of Scale," 268, and Los Angeles map on 269)

D. Built environment and social space
    1. Transportation and infrastructure (232, 298, 299)
    2. Political organization of urban areas (While this sub-topic is not directly addressed in the text, the broad frameworks of urban politics are covered in Chapter 25, "Political Change and the Evolving State," 338-54. Students will find it beneficial

to review this section of the text. The introduction and the section on "Political Culture" will be particularly timely as well, 338-41.)

    3. Locational decisions, conflicts, and hazards (241-44)

    4. Uneven development, ghettoization, and gentrification (267-69)

    5. Patterns of race, ethnicity, gender, and class (Chapters 30 and 31 provide a comprehensive treatment of these issues, 418-48)

    6. Impacts of suburbanization and edge cities* (269-70)

E. Responses to urban growth

    1. Urban planning and design (The section on "Revitalizing the Center" in Chapter 20, 267-69 examines this sub-topic but not specifically in these precise terms. In addition, the Atlanta case study in "Focus On," 271, explores planning and design issues affecting a major American city.)

    2. Community action and initiatives (This is an open-ended topic not typically covered in human geography textbooks. It can be best explored through case studies on selected local issues - e.g., community policing, urban block clubs, neighborhood action groups, local school councils, etc. - as well as through research investigations of similar issues affecting cities beyond the United States.)

* Because "Edge City" is a relatively recent term in the vocabulary of urban geography, it is not yet discussed in most urban geography textbooks. Edge cities are largely an American phenomena of the late twentieth century and identify satellites of such old and established cities as Boston, Chicago, New York, San Francisco, etc. These new urban inventions are characterized by corporate parks, shopping malls, complexes of motels and hotels, convention centers, entertainment cores, and subdivisions of single family homes. Originally rural village centers set up to service local truck farmers, these curious new urban cores now ring the great cities through freeway connections and easy access routes to a major regional or international airport.

For a full treatment of the topic, refer to: Joel Garreau, Edge City: Life on the New Frontier. New York: Doubleday. 1991.

E. Topic VII Study Questions - Cities and Urban Land Use

1. Describe the difference between site and situation as each relates to urban location
2. Discuss the role of the "world city." Why is it a twentieth century phenomenon?
3. Identify the varieties of design in ancient cities. Explain the reasons for the variations.
4. What are the characteristics of the primate city?
5.   What are the differences among mercantile cities, manufacturing cities, and modern cities?
6. Explain the relationship between social stratification and urban elites.
7. Why are urban places ranked?
8. What are hinterlands? Explain the role they play in the organization of urban places.
9. Give several reasons explaining why megalopolises exist the modern world.
10. Distinguish between a megacity and a megalopolis.
11. Analyze the significance of Christaller's central place theory.
12. What made urban planning attractive to many city officials and civic groups in the United States in the early twentieth century?
13. Explain how cities in Africa, Latin America and Asia differ from those in North America and Europe.
14. Analyze the positive and negative impacts of urban gentrification.
15. What factors explain both agglomeration and deglomeration in the rise and decline of cities?

F. Researching Topic VII - Cities and Urban Land Use

Students will find that preparing short research papers (i.e., up to five pages) as part of the study of a topic is an effective means of deepening their understanding of its meaning and purpose within the realm of human geography. Such research serves not only as an introduction to the resources available about the topic but also as a strategy for applying the skills of organization and presentation essential to responding to the extended answer questions on the Advanced Placement examination in Human Geography.

The topics provided here are certainly not comprehensive and all-inclusive, but only serve as suggestions for the kind of research and investigation students can undertake. Each research paper should be written from an outline developed from the student's research with a brief introduction stating the hypothesis (i.e., a tentative explanation that accounts for a set of facts that will be tested by the investigation presented in the paper). A hypothesis, then, is merely a theory or a speculation that the researcher sets out to prove or disprove.

The body of the research paper provides the detail addressing the hypothesis. It provides precise information derived from the research the student has done and also follows the outline that has been prepared. As a result, the arguments should be well organized and logically presented. Including anecdotes and examples will make the paper more convincing and also more persuasive.

The final part of the research paper is the conclusion. That is the section providing a summary of what the student has argued and joins those arguments to the hypothesis. The purpose of the conclusion is to demonstrate why the hypothesis works (or does not work). It is the part of the paper where the writer rests the case.

To be convincing, research papers should contain citations and bibliographies. That gives them credibility and it also helps validate the arguments the student presents. Because there is no *one* correct way to document research these days, teachers will provide the necessary guidance and direction for students. There are several widely used style manuals available. However, the three most often used to guide reporting research in human geography include:

American Psychological Association. *Publication Manual of the American Psychological Association.* 4th ed. Washington, D. C.: American Psychological Association. 1994.

Gibaldi, Joseph *MLA Handbook for Writers of Research Papers.* 4th ed. New York: Modern Language Association. 1995.

The Chicago Manual of Style. 14th ed. Chicago: University of Chicago Press. 1993.

Some Suggested Research Topics for Cities and Urban Land Use

A Non-Western Urban Model: A Case Study
Cities as Economic Entities
Hexagons and Honeycombs: Christaller's "Central Places"
Models of Urban Development: A Critical Analysis
Patterns of Urban Hierarchies: Studies in Diffusion
Racial Segregation in American Cities: An Historical Overview
Suburban Development in the United States
The Postmodern City: Some Predictions and Speculations
Ancient and Modern Athens: A Comparative Analysis
Urban Planning and the "Ideal City"
Why the Megalopolis?

G. Connecting to *Human Geography in Action*

Chapter 9 (9-1 to 9-22 plus CD) introduces students to both central place theory and the structure of urban hierarchies by providing both clear explanations and practical application activities. Students will learn about the threshold of a function by examining the relationship between the size of a city and the number of pizza parlors it is able to support (9--9 to 9-13) and the difference between low-order and high-order central place functions by evaluating maps showing the distribution of major and minor league baseball teams. The maps in this exercise are generated by a Geographic Information System (GIS).

In Chapter 10 (10-1 to 10-16), students develop single-page profiles of census tracts based on statistics gathered from government documents. The activity also provides opportunities to learn about "edge cities" and how they function. Figure 10.3 (10-5) uses metropolitan Philadelphia as a case in point to illustrate this emerging phenomenon.

H. Sample Multiple-Choice Questions

These questions are typical of the kinds of questions students can expect on the examination in Advanced Placement Human Geography. Reviewing the section on multiple-choice questions in Chapter 3 will help students better orient themselves for selecting the appropriate answer in the sample questions included here.

Directions: Each of the questions or incomplete statements is followed by five suggested answers or completions.. Select the one that is best in each case.

1. Which of the following has most affected the development of suburbs in the United States in the last 50 years?
    A. popularity of the automobile
    B. inexpensive and reliable electrical energy
    C. computer technology and the internet
    D. high-speed rail transportation
    E. access to regional airports

2. What statement best characterizes a feature of the concentric zone model of urban development?
    A. A multi-metropolitan complex is formed by the coalescence of two or more major urban areas.
    B. Urban growth conforms to sectors radiating out from the downtown along such transportation routes as bus and train lines.
    C. The city is organized into groupings of specialized activities (e.g., housing districts, shopping areas, port facilities, etc.).
    D. The central business district (CBD) is the focus of the city's social, commercial, and civic life.
    E. City growth is haphazard following no particular design or predictable formula of development.

3. Which of the following economic activities is most likely to be found in a city's central business district (CBD)?
    A. an automobile dealership
    B. a transfer point for railroad freight cars
    C. an office tower
    D. a metal fabricating plant
    E. the production facility of a major textbook publisher

Note: Use the following essay to answer questions 4 through 7.

Urban Growth in the Netherlands

The Netherlands is one of the most densely populated countries in Europe. Most of the people live in its highly urbanized western part - an area known as the Randstad. The Randstad includes two dense population clusters. In the north are the cities of Haarlem, Amsterdam, Hilversum, and Utrecht; in the south there are Leyden, The Hague, Rotterdam, and Dordrecht. Between these two urban groupings is a line of continuous settlement but that area is less densely populated. It is called the Green Heart.

Over the years, the urban growth of the Randstad has been significant. Less than a hundred years ago, its cities were quite small and set far apart from one another. By 1900, as a result of the impact of the Industrial Revolution, the population of the cities rapidly increased. As the economy of the Netherlands developed, tens of thousands of job opportunities became available, and people poured into the growing urban clusters from the country's rural areas.

Within fifty years, the Randstad had become a huge urban complex. The growth was expected to continue for many more years, but by 1960, the number of people living in the four largest cities had begun to decline. Growth was spilling over into the suburban areas of the Green Heart. People left for a number of reasons. Many of the older homes had become hazardous and uncomfortable. The need for space for new office buildings, hotels, and assembly facilities meant that old structures were torn down. This decreased the housing supply. Thus people were attracted to the greenery of the suburbs away from the noise and traffic that had become a part of urban life.

4. What is the term urban geographers use to identify the settlement patterns that have developed since industrialization in the Randstad and the population growth in the Green Heart?
   A. urban core
   B. metropolis
   C. protruded areas
   D. central business district
   E. megalopolis

5. What accounted for the growth of the Randstad after 1900?
   A. increasing job opportunities in the cities
   B. decline in agricultural production
   C. dam and dike programs to control flooding
   D. rapid development of affordable housing in urban areas
   E. improved transport systems connecting the Randstad with the Green Heart

6. Why did many people leave the urban centers of the Randstad in the 1960s?
   A. The economy weakened resulting in massive layoffs.
   B. The Dutch government intervened to control the growth of cities.
   C. The demand for commercial space caused a housing shortage.
   D. Transportation networks made outlying areas more accessible.
   E. The Dutch economy became more dispersed due to changing patterns of trade.

7. Human geographers identify the attractive features of the Green Heart that encouraged migration away from the core cities of the Randstad as
    A. push factors.
    B. pull factors.
    C. gentrification.
    D. threshold of function.
    E. travel effort.

8. On what principle is the hierarchy of urban places primarily based?
    A. population and their function and services
    B. their site and situation
    C. the availability of customized services
    D. the dominance of a single downtown serving as the urban core
    E. the number of basic industries providing job opportunities

9. Compare Figure 18-7 (248) to Figure 24.3 (330) to identify the statement identifying the most appropriate relationship established by the data on the two maps.
    A. The data presented is so inconsistent and contradictory that no valid relationship can be drawn.
    B. There is a high correlation between cities that have populations beyond 15 million and those serving major global financial roles.
    C. World cities and those with large populations tend to cluster in the southern hemisphere.
    D. Population size has little impact on the financial role a city plays in the world economy.
    E. Africa and most of Asia and the Pacific Rim play no role in the world economy.

10. All of the following account for the success of modern urban centers except
    A. their external locational attributes.
    B. their relative location with reference to non-local places.
    C. the physical qualities of the areas they occupy.
    D. their distance from other urban centers.
    E. their relatively easy access to other places.

Answers: 1) A 2) D 3) C 4) E 5) A 6) C 7) B 8) A 9) B 10) C

I. Sample Free-Response Questions

These questions are similar to the free-response items likely to be on the Advanced Placement Human Geography examination.

1. Describe a hinterland and explain why it is important in determining the hierarchies of urban places.

2. Evaluate the positive and negative factors that influence a city's site and situation. Provide examples to illustrate the points you make.

3. Compare the preindustrial city with the emerging model of the postmodern city.

4. Describe the characteristics of a primate city.

5. Explain why role and function are determining factors in a city's success.

Chapter 12

Selected Readings: Anticipating Advanced Placement Human Geography

For many students, Advanced Placement Human Geography will be their first geography experience since elementary or middle school. For some, their likely recollection is a geography program organized around memorizing places on the map and matching capitals with states and countries, products with their places of origin, and major cities and regions with countries and continents. Although helpful in developing a mental map of Earth, such an exposure to geography is not very informative about the planet's physical and human systems and their interaction. Nor does it promote an awareness of the connections between and among places, or an understanding of the world in spatial terms. As valuable as the earlier school study might have been in promoting a core understanding of geography, the perspective was probably quite basic and narrow and not focused on promoting a view of the world that described the changing patterns of places or methods for unraveling their meaning.

Thus this reading list. The books on it have been selected to help students understand the nature and complexity of geography before undertaking its formal study in the Advanced Placement Human Geography program. They will serve as an introduction to all the realms of geography but with a special emphasis on the elements of human geography. In its own way, each book will broaden students' knowledge of the discipline by helping make the complex simple, and the intricate interesting.

The list is quite eclectic. Each book offers an insight to what human geography is and how human geographers analyze and interpret the world. The books have been selected because they are easily accessible, eminently readable, broadly informative, and specifically focused on some important aspect of human geography such as urban development or religion and culture. Students who read from this list in anticipation of their Advanced Placement Human Geography course will not only enjoy the subject matter of the books they select but also develop a context that will make their Advanced Placement experience more meaningful.

Davis, Kenneth C. *Don't Know Much about Geography: Everything You Need to Know about the World but Never Learned* (New York: William Morrow and Company, Inc., 1992). The author uses this book to popularize geography by making it a lively and fascinating inquiry on places, personalities, and events - but always in a spatial context. Written with humor and insight, Davis explains how geography plays a key role in shaping the destiny of nations and regions. He gives special emphasis to toponyms (i.e., the origin and meaning of place names) as a means of helping his readers understand Earth's complexity.

de Blij, H. J., *Harm de Blij's Geography Book: A Leading Geographer's Fresh Look at Our Changing World* (New York: John Wiley and Sons, Inc., 1995).
The author of the text for which the **Study Guide** has been prepared has provided a concise and focused overview of geography - what it is, how a knowledge of it is essential for understanding contemporary issues, and how it can be applied to inform the world view of Americans. Rich in interpretations of the physical and human phenomena of Earth, de Blij has included valuable insights (and anecdotes) on the role geography plays in illuminating today's political, economic, and social problems.

Demko, George J. with Agel, Jerome, and Boe, Eugene *Why in the World: Adventures in Geography* (New York: Doubleday/Anchor Books, 1992).
The authors entertainingly demonstrate that geography provides a multi-faceted look at the never-ending drama between the world's physical and cultural environments. It is an engaging introduction to the "new" geography that demonstrates how the physical and social sciences,

and the humanities are joined through the lens of geography. The book also includes the biographies of 173 of the world's countries.

Garreau, Joel *Edge City: Life on the New Frontier* (New York: Doubleday, 1991).
Garreau is a journalist, not a geographer, but in this exquisite monograph about new urban expressions, he shows the practical applications of geography to help his readers understand the way Americans have dramatically changed their cities in the late twentieth century. The book is a convincing study about the importance of the uses of human geography.

Hanson, Susan, ed. *Ten Geographic Ideas that Changed the World* (New Brunswick: Rutgers University Press, 1997).
In a series of thought-provoking and often witty essays, some of the most distinguished geographers in the United States explore and explain ten geographic ideas that have literally changed the world. They examine such topics as the power of maps in our lives as well as the importance of how and why we perceive places the way we do. The collection is an excellent introduction to modern geography.

Sherer, Thomas E., Jr. *The Complete Idiot's Guide™ to Geography* (New York: Alpha Books, 1997).
Even though the title of this book seems a bit impish, it provides solid information about the world and its regions, and how people and places interact. Through an extensive use of maps, the author helps the reader understand the why of where using trivia tidbits, anecdotes, and interesting descriptions of the history, culture and customs of each of the world's culture realms.

Tuan, Yi Fu *Passing Strange and Wonderful: Aesthetics, Nature and Culture* (Washington, D.C.: Island Press, 1993).
Beginning with the individual and the physical world, the author explores human progress from the simple to the complex. As a human geographer of great sensitivity and insight, Tuan subtly examines the moral and ethical aspects of the discipline. To guide his readers to a fuller understanding of human experience, he describes how the aesthetic operates in four widely disparate cultures: Australian aboriginal, Chinese, medieval European, and modern American.

Supplemental Resources

In addition to these introductions to human geography, there are other resources that will be valuable tools in the study of Advanced Placement Human Geography. This list identifies books that students can use to supplement *Human Geography: Culture, Society, and Space.* (Sixth Edition).

Espenshade, Edward B., Jr. ed. *Goode's World Atlas* (19th ed.) (Chicago: Rand McNally, 1995).
This is a comprehensive atlas that is well indexed for the easy location of thousands of the world's places. It is regionally organized but also contains sections of major city maps, thematic maps, and geographical tables.

Goodall. Brian *The Penguin Dictionary of Human Geography* (London: Penguin, 1987).
This book contains a glossary of terms necessary for a full understanding of the vocabulary special to the study of human geography.

Kapit, Wynn *The Geography Coloring Book* (New York: Harper Collins, 1991).

This unique, hands-on resource introduces students to the array of the world's regions by helping them visualize the location of places. Included for each of the maps to be colored is essential data (e.g., population, type of government, official language, predominant religions, etc.). The maps are simple in outline and detail and thus easy to use.

Webster's New Geographical Dictionary (Springfield, MA: Merriam-Webster, Inc. Publishers, 1988)
The thousands of entries in this reference volume provide basic information on the world's countries, regions, cities, and natural features. More than two hundred maps are also included.

TAKE NOTE!

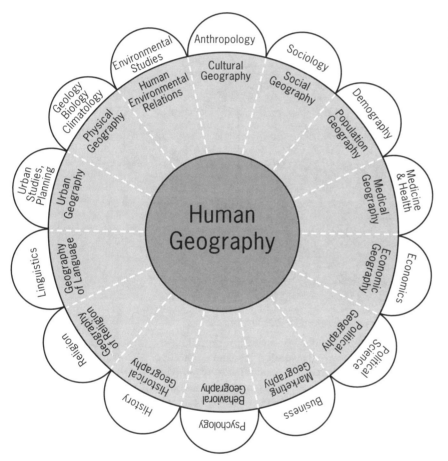

Figure 1-1 Fields of Human Geography. A schematic diagram showing the relationships among the fields of human geography and related fields outside the discipline. *Source: From authors' sketch.*

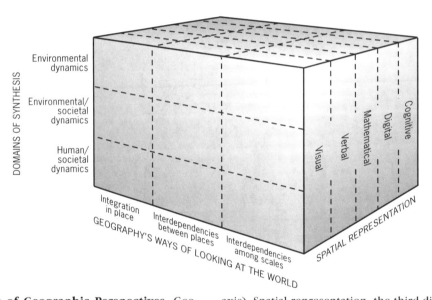

Figure 1-2 Matrix of Geographic Perspectives. Geography's ways of looking at the world—through its focus on place and scale (horizontal axis)—cuts across its three domains of synthesis: human-societal dynamics, environmental dynamics, and environmental-societal dynamics (vertical axis). Spatial representation, the third dimension of the matrix, underpins and sometimes drives research in other branches of geography. *Source: National Research Council, 1997*. Rediscovering Geography: New Relevance for Science and Society. *Washington, D.C.: National Academy Press.*

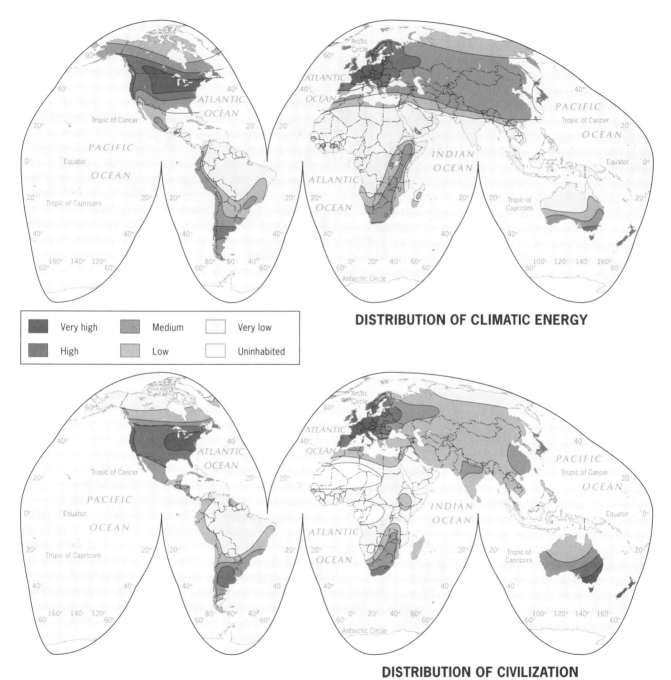

DISTRIBUTION OF CLIMATIC ENERGY

Very high　　Medium　　Very low

High　　Low　　Uninhabited

DISTRIBUTION OF CIVILIZATION

Figure 2-9 Distribution of Climatic Energy and of Civilization. This is how E. Huntington viewed climate and civilization. Below these maps, the author states that they are "based on the opinion of fifty experts in many countries." *Source: E. Huntington*, Principles of Human Geography. *New York: Wiley, 1940, p. 352.*

　　　93

Figure 3-6 Global Terrain. Despite centuries of technological progress, the influence of terrain as an element of the overall natural environment still is reflected in world population distribution. Mountains and high plateaus do not generally support large or dense population clusters.

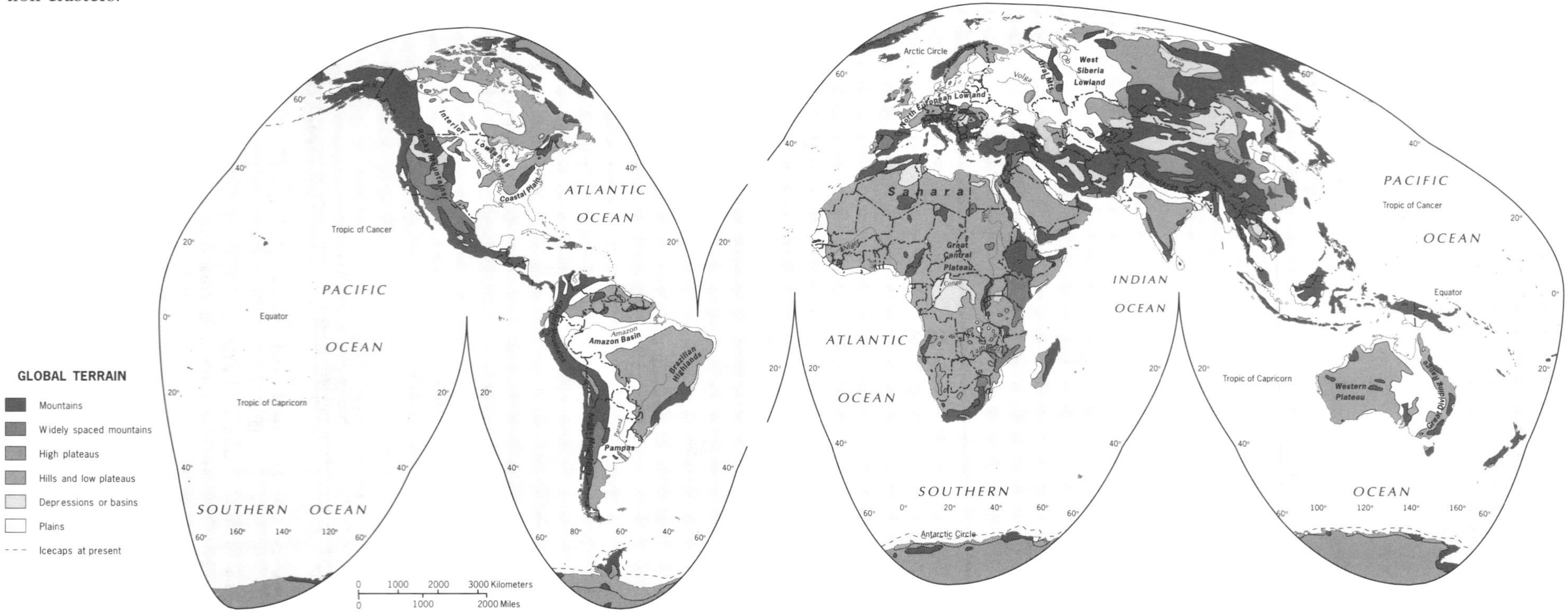

94

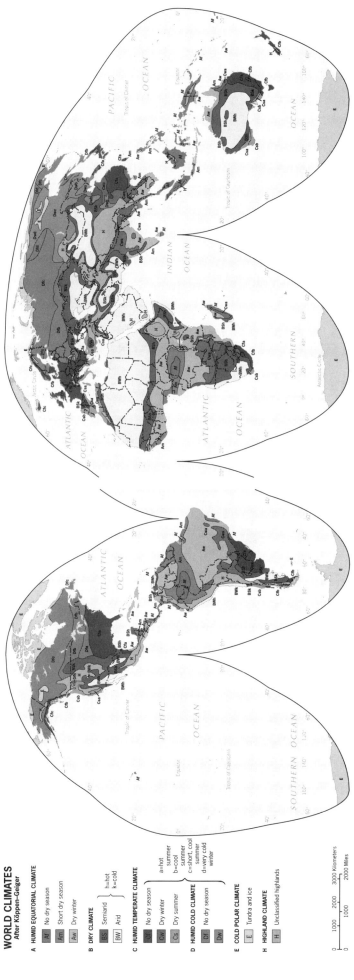

Figure 3-7 World Climates. The Köppen map of world climates as modified by R. Geiger. These, of course, are macroclimatic regions; microclimates are set within these but cannot be shown at this scale.

WORLD CLIMATES
After Köppen–Geiger

A HUMID EQUATORIAL CLIMATE

Af   No dry season

Am   Short dry season

Aw   Dry winter

B DRY CLIMATE

BS   Semiarid   h=hot
BW   Arid   k=cold

C HUMID TEMPERATE CLIMATE

Cf   No dry season
Cw   Dry winter   a=hot summer
Cs   Dry summer   b=cool summer
                         c=short, cool summer
D HUMID COLD CLIMATE   d=very cold winter

Df   No dry season
Dw   Dry season

E COLD POLAR CLIMATE

E   Tundra and ice

H HIGHLAND CLIMATE

H   Unclassified highlands

0   1000   2000   3000 Kilometers
0   1000   2000 Miles

Table 4-1 Population Densities for Selected Countries, 1998

Country	1995 Population (millions)	Area (thousand sq mi/km)	Arithmetic Density (sq mi/km)	Physiologic Density (sq mi/km)
Egypt	66.2	386.7/1001.6	172/66	8161/3150
Japan	126.5	145.7/377.4	870/335	6788/2620
Netherlands	15.6	15.9/41.2	981/379	4431/1711
Bangladesh	124.6	55.6/144.0	2478/956	3779/1459
Colombia	38.2	439.7/1138.8	87/34	1709/660
India	988.1	1237.1/3204.1	798/308	1491/576
Nigeria	110.3	356.7/923.9	309/119	901/348
Argentina	36.0	1068.3/2766.9	34/14	689/266
United States	269.3	3787.4/9808.4	71/27	367/142

Sources: Calculated from World Population Data Sheet published by the Population Reference Bureau, Inc., from data on agriculture in the Encyclopaedia Britannica *Book of the Year* 1997, and from the United Nations Food and Agriculture Organization (FAO) *Production Yearbook* 1996. Note that population data in this table may not correspond to statistics drawn from other sources. (See "Focus on: Reliability of Population Data.")

Figure 4-1 World Population Distribution.

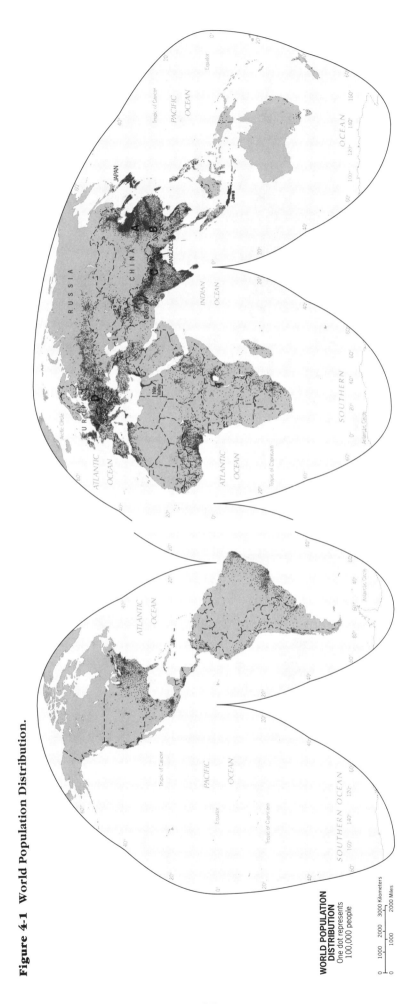

**WORLD POPULATION
DISTRIBUTION**
One dot represents
100,000 people

Figure 4-2 World Population Density.

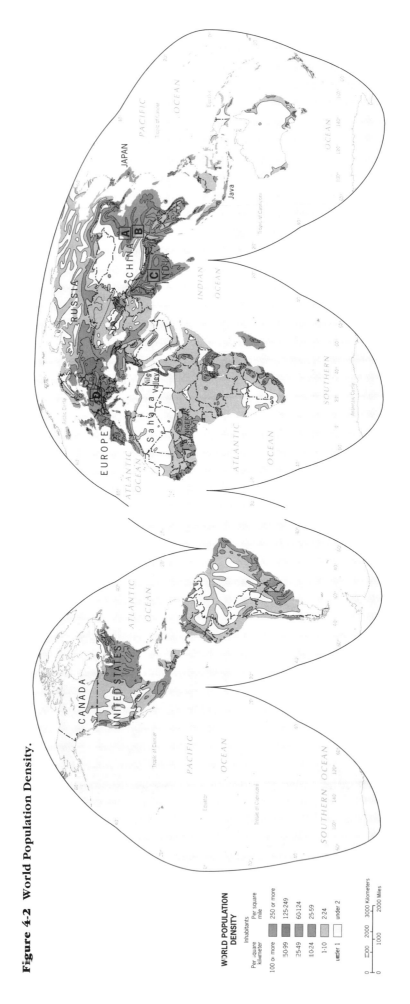

WORLD POPULATION DENSITY

Per square kilometer	Per square mile
100 or more	250 or more
50-99	125-249
25-49	60-124
10-24	25-59
1-10	2-24
under 1	under 2

Inhabitants

0   1000   2000   3000 Kilometers
0   1000   2000 Miles

98   *Copyright © 2000 John Wiley & Sons, Inc.*

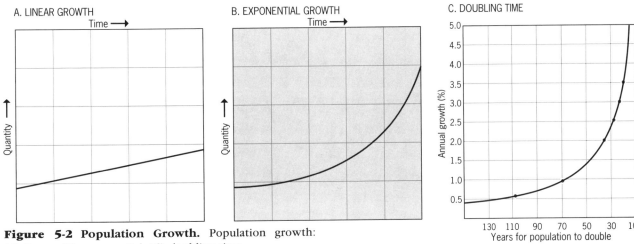

Figure 5-2 Population Growth. Population growth:
(A) linear; (B) exponential; (C) doubling time.

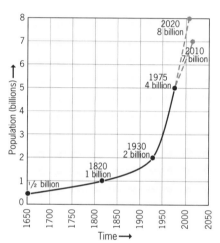

Figure 5-3 Population Growth, 1650 to (estimated) 2020. The dotted lines indicate different scenarios depending on birth rate trends in the coming decades.

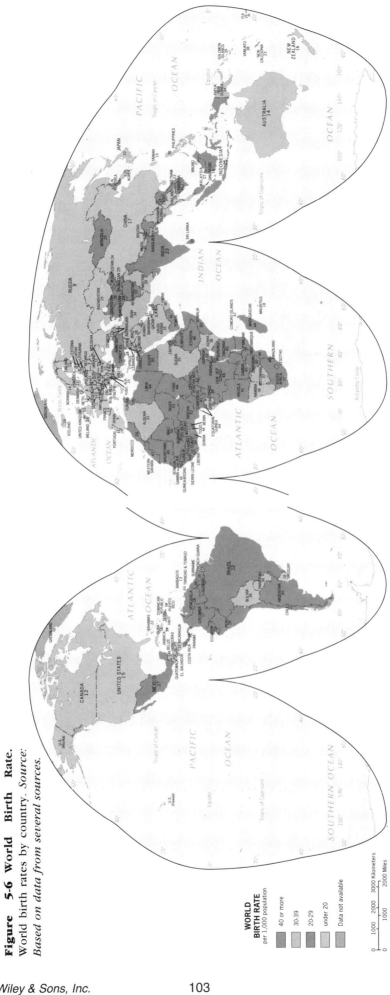

Figure 5-6 World Birth Rate.
World birth rates by country. *Source: Based on data from several sources.*

WORLD
BIRTH RATE
per 1,000 population

- 40 or more
- 30-39
- 20-29
- under 20
- Data not available

0 1000 2000 3000 Kilometers
0   1000   2000 Miles

103

Figure 5-7 World Mortality Rate.
World death rates by country. *Source:*
Based on data from several sources.

**WORLD
MORTALITY RATE**
deaths per 1,000 population

- 20 or more
- 10-19
- Under 10
- Data not available

1000   2000   3000 Kilometers
1000   2000 Miles

104

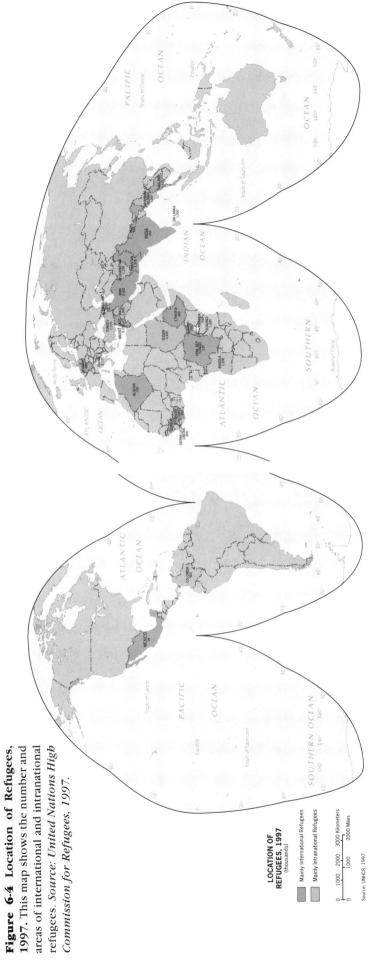

Figure 6-4 Location of Refugees,
1997. This map shows the number and
areas of international and intranational
refugees. *Source: United Nations High
Commission for Refugees, 1997.*

**LOCATION OF
REFUGEES, 1997**
(thousands)

Mainly International Refugees

Mainly Intranational Refugees

0   1000   2000   3000 Kilometers
0   1000   2000 Miles

Source: UNHCR, 1997

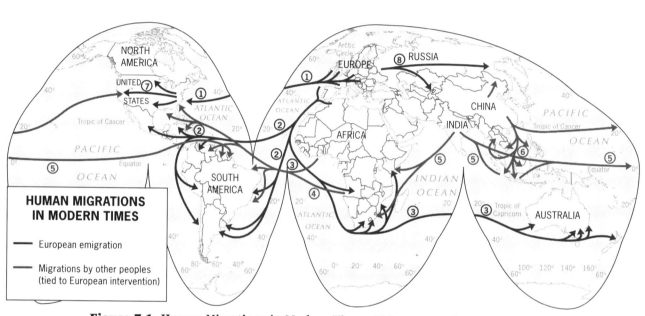

Figure 7-1 Human Migrations in Modern Times. Major routes of migrants.

Figure 8-2 Language Families of the World. Generalized map of the world distribution of language families. *Source: Based on a map prepared by Hammond, Inc., for the first edition, 1977.*

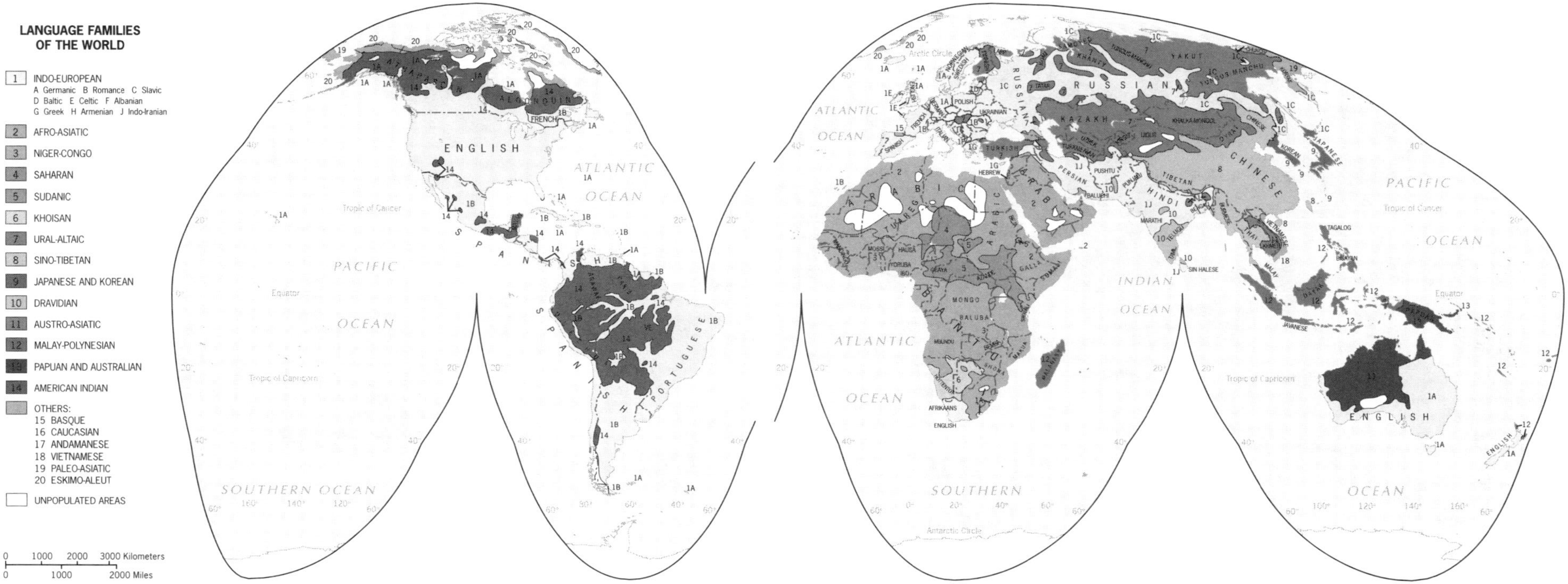
LANGUAGE FAMILIES OF THE WORLD
1 INDO-EUROPEAN
A Germanic B Romance C Slavic
D Baltic E Celtic F Albanian
G Greek H Armenian J Indo-Iranian
2 AFRO-ASIATIC
3 NIGER-CONGO
4 SAHARAN
5 SUDANIC
6 KHOISAN
7 URAL-ALTAIC
8 SINO-TIBETAN
9 JAPANESE AND KOREAN
10 DRAVIDIAN
11 AUSTRO-ASIATIC
12 MALAY-POLYNESIAN
13 PAPUAN AND AUSTRALIAN
14 AMERICAN INDIAN
OTHERS:
15 BASQUE
16 CAUCASIAN
17 ANDAMANESE
18 VIETNAMESE
19 PALEO-ASIATIC
20 ESKIMO-ALEUT
UNPOPULATED AREAS
0 1000 2000 3000 Kilometers
0 1000 2000 Miles
ENGLISH
ALGONQUIN
FRENCH
SPANISH
PORTUGUESE
ATLANTIC OCEAN
PACIFIC OCEAN
SOUTHERN OCEAN
INDIAN OCEAN
Tropic of Cancer
Tropic of Capricorn
Equator
Arctic Circle
Antarctic Circle
RUSSIAN
KAZAKH
YAKUT
CHINESE
TIBETAN
HINDI
PERSIAN
PUSHTU
TURKISH
HEBREW
ARABIC
MONGO
BALUBA
AFRIKAANS
TAGALOG
JAVANESE
MALAY
JAPANESE
KOREAN
SIN HALESE
MARATHI
POLISH
UKRAINIAN

LANGUAGES OF EUROPE
0 200 400 600 Kilometers
0 100 200 300 Miles
Arctic Circle
Norwegian Sea
ATLANTIC OCEAN
North Sea
Mediterranean Sea
Black Sea
Icelandic
Faeroese
Saami
Samoyedic
Karelian
Finnish
Swedish
Norwegian
Russian
Scots Gaelic
English
Irish Gaelic
Welsh
Estonian
Latvian
Lithuanian
Danish
Frisian
Dutch
German
Belarusian
Polish
Ukrainian
Breton
Alsatian
Czech
Slovak
French
Romanian
Hungarian
Slovene
Galician
Basque
Provençal
Italian
Serbo-Croatian
Bulgarian
Macedonian
Albanian
Catalan
Portuguese
Spanish
Greek
Turkish
Major Indo-European Branches
Germanic group
WESTERN GERMANIC
NORTHERN GERMANIC
1 Dutch
2 German
3 Frisian
4 English
5 Danish
6 Swedish
7 Norwegian
8 Icelandic
9 Faeroses
Romance group
10 Portuguese
11 Spanish
12 Catalan
13 Provençal
14 French
15 Italian
16 Rhaeto-Romance
17 Romanian
Slavic group
WEST SLAVONIC
EAST SLAVONIC
SOUTH SLAVONIC
18 Polish
19 Slovak
20 Czech
21 Sorbian
22 Russian
23 Ukrainian
24 Belarusian
25 Slovene
26 Serbo-Croatian
27 Macedonian
28 Bulgarian
Other Indo-European Branches
Celtic group
BRITTANIC
GAULISH
29 Breton
30 Welsh
31 Irish Gaelic
32 Scots Gaelic
Baltic group
33 Lativian
34 Lithuanian
Hellenic
35 Greek
Thracian/Illyrian group
36 Albanian
Thracian/Illyrian group
37 Romani
Uralic Language Family
Finno-Ugric group
38 Ginnish
39 Karelian
40 Saami
41 Estonian
42 Hungarian
Samoyedic group
44 Samoyedic
Altaic Language Family
Turkic group
45 Turkish
Other Languages
Basque
46 Basque
Areas with significant concentrations of other languages (usually adjacent national langueages).
Boundary between languages.
Boundary between Indo-European and non-Indo-European languages.

Figure 8-3 Languages of Europe. Generalized map of language-use regions in Europe. *Source: Based on a map in Murphy, A. B. 1998 "European Languages," T. Unwin, ed.,* A European Geography. *London: Longman.*

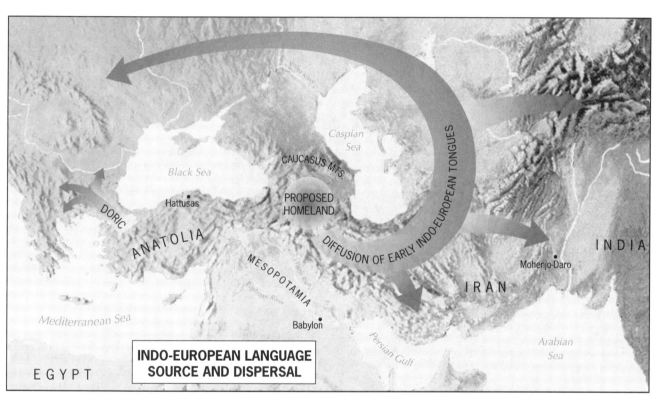

Figure 9-2 Indo-European Language Source and Dispersal. Postulated diffusion of an Indo-European proto-language. *Source: From T. V. Gamkrelidze and V. V. Ivanov, Scientific American, March 1990, p. 112.*

119

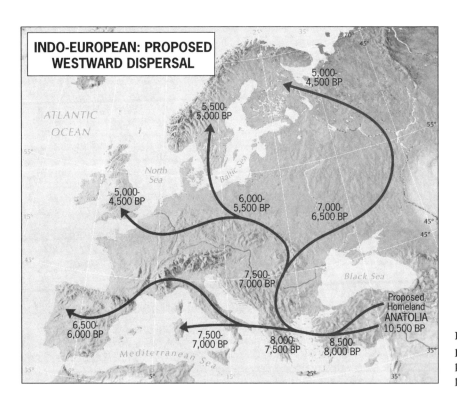

INDO-EUROPEAN: PROPOSED
WESTWARD DISPERSAL

ATLANTIC
OCEAN

North
Sea

Baltic Sea

5,000-
4,500 BP

5,500-
5,000 BP

6,000-
5,500 BP

7,000-
6,500 BP

5,000-
4,500 BP

Black Sea

7,500-
7,000 BP

Proposed
Homeland
ANATOLIA
10,500 BP

6,500-
6,000 BP

7,500-
7,000 BP

8,000-
7,500 BP

8,500-
8,000 BP

Mediterranean Sea

Figure 9-3 Indo-European Proposed Westward Dispersal. The approximate timing of the westward dispersal of the Indo-European languages.

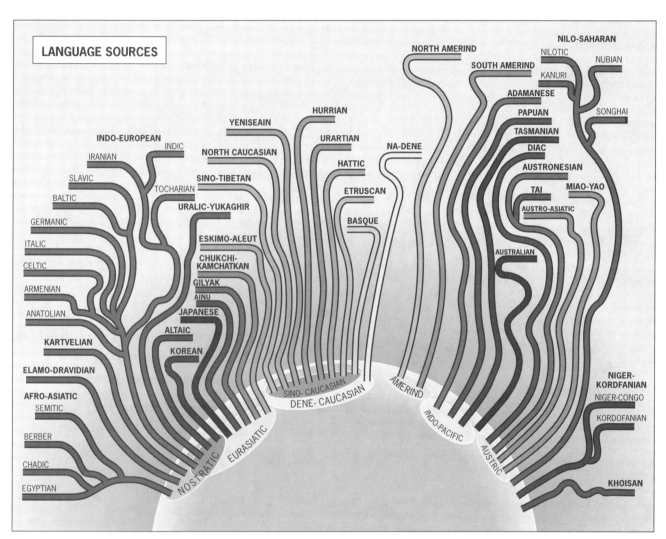

Figure 9-4 Language Sources. *Source: After a diagram in Philip E. Ross, "Hard Words,"* Scientific American, *April 1991, p. 139.*

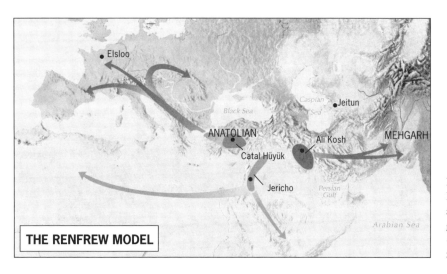

Figure 9-5 The Renfrew Model. The Renfrew Model poses that three source areas of agriculture each gave rise to a great language family. *Source: From "The Origins of Indo-European Languages,"* Scientific American, *1989, p. 114.*

Figure 13-3 Two Exclaves in Transcaucasia. This map shows two Transcaucasian exclaves: Muslim-Azerbaijan Nakhichevan, cut off by Christian Armenia, and Christian-Armenian Nagorno-Karabakh, surrounded by Muslim Azerbaijan.

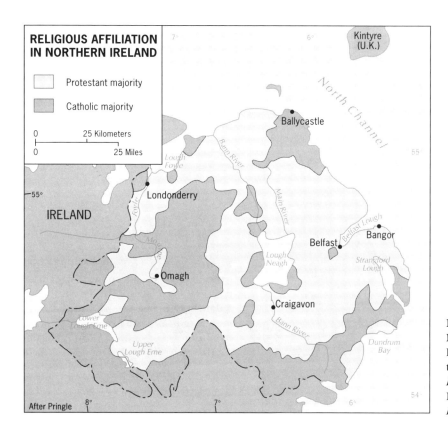

Figure 13-5 Religious Affiliation in Northern Ireland. Areas of Catholic and Protestant majorities are scattered throughout Northern Ireland. *Source: From D. G. Pringle*, One Island, Two Nations? *Letchworth: Research Studies Press/Wiley, 1985, p. 21.*

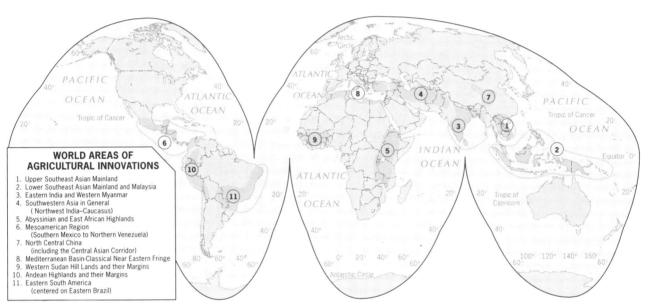

WORLD AREAS OF AGRICULTURAL INNOVATIONS

1. Upper Southeast Asian Mainland
2. Lower Southeast Asian Mainland and Malaysia
3. Eastern India and Western Myanmar
4. Southwestern Asia in General
   (Northwest India–Caucasus)
5. Abyssinian and East African Highlands
6. Mesoamerican Region
   (Southern Mexico to Northern Venezuela)
7. North Central China
   (including the Central Asian Corridor)
8. Mediterranean Basin-Classical Near Eastern Fringe
9. Western Sudan Hill Lands and their Margins
10. Andean Highlands and their Margins
11. Eastern South America
    (centered on Eastern Brazil)

Figure 14-2 World Areas of Agricultural Innovations. Cultural geographer Carl Sauer identified 11 areas where agricultural innovations occurred. *Source: From C. O. Sauer*, Agricultural Origins and Dispersals. *New York: American Geographical Society, 1952, p. 24.*

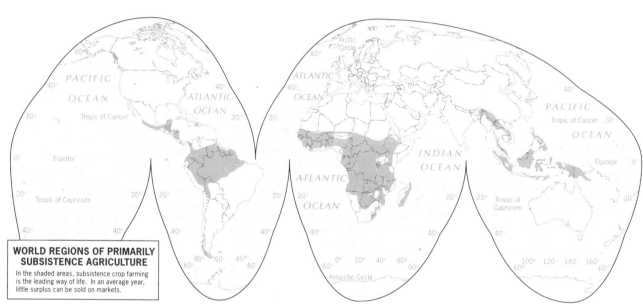

**WORLD REGIONS OF PRIMARILY
SUBSISTENCE AGRICULTURE**

In the shaded areas, subsistence crop farming
is the leading way of life. In an average year,
little surplus can be sold on markets.

Figure 14-3 World Regions of Primarily Subsistence Agriculture. Definitions of
subsistence farming vary. India and China are not shaded because farmers sell some produce on markets; in equatorial Africa and South America, subsistence allows little of this.

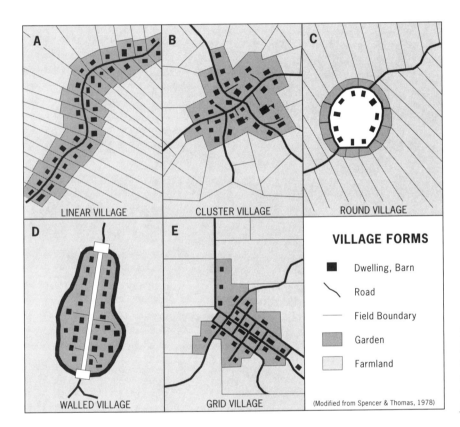

A

LINEAR VILLAGE

B

CLUSTER VILLAGE

C

ROUND VILLAGE

D

WALLED VILLAGE

E

GRID VILLAGE

VILLAGE FORMS

■   Dwelling, Barn

╱   Road

—   Field Boundary

  Garden

  Farmland

(Modified from Spencer & Thomas, 1978)

Figure 15-3 Village Forms. Five different representative village layouts are shown here. *Source: From J. E. Spencer and W. H. Thomas,* Introducing Cultural Geography. *New York: Wiley, 1978, p. 154.*

Figure 16-1 World Agriculture. Different kinds of agricultural areas are shown through the world. *Source: From a map prepared by Hammond, Inc. for the first edition, 1977.*

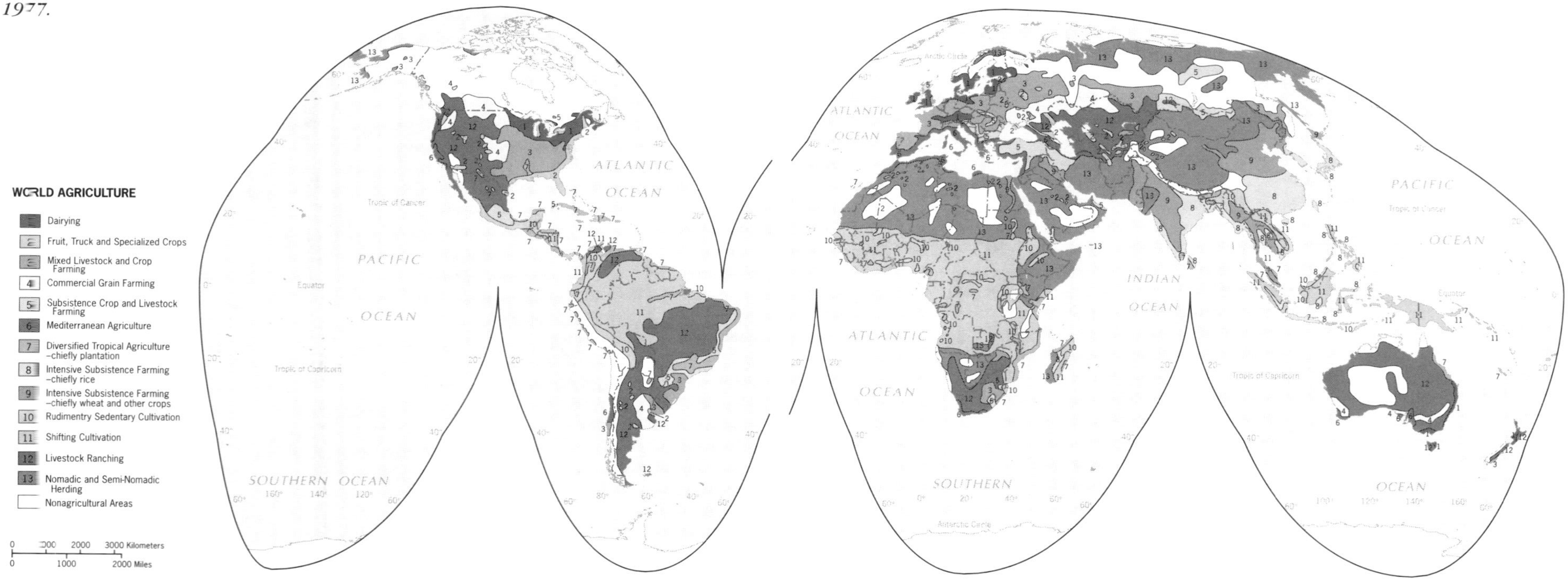

WORLD AGRICULTURE

1. Dairying
2. Fruit, Truck and Specialized Crops
3. Mixed Livestock and Crop Farming
4. Commercial Grain Farming
5. Subsistence Crop and Livestock Farming
6. Mediterranean Agriculture
7. Diversified Tropical Agriculture —chiefly plantation
8. Intensive Subsistence Farming —chiefly rice
9. Intensive Subsistence Farming —chiefly wheat and other crops
10. Rudimentry Sedentary Cultivation
11. Shifting Cultivation
12. Livestock Ranching
13. Nomadic and Semi-Nomadic Herding

Nonagricultural Areas

0 500 1000 2000 3000 Kilometers
0 1000 2000 Miles

Figure 17-2 Maya and Aztec America. This map indicates early centers of culture in Maya and Aztec America.

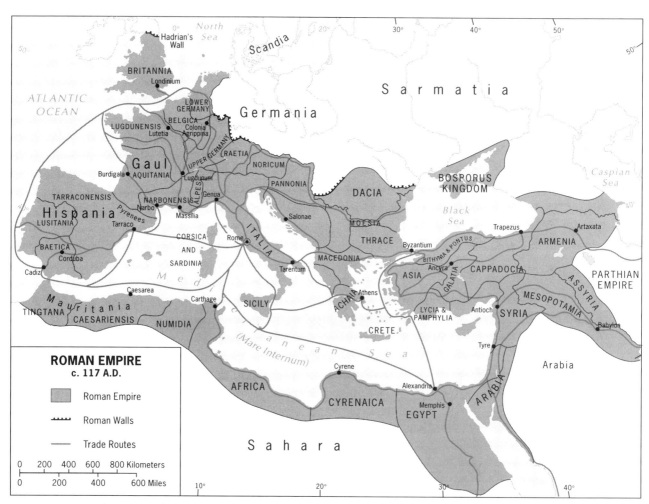

Figure 17-4 **The Roman Empire, circa 117 A.D.** The Romans established a system of cities linked by a network of land and sea routes. Many of the Roman cities have grown into modern metropolises.

Figure 18-2 Xianggang–Shenzhen. Shenzhen, China's most successful Special Economic Zone, lies adjacent to Xianggang (Hong Kong), one of the economic "tigers" of the Pacific Rim. This proximity has propelled Shenzhen's SEZ ahead of all others. *Source: From a map in H. J. de Blij and P. O. Muller, Geography: Realms, Regions, and Concepts, 8th ed. New York: Wiley, 1997).*

Figure 18-6 Urban Population as a Percentage of the Total Population. *Source: Data from Population Reference Bureau, World Population Data Sheet 1998. Washington, D.C., 1998.*

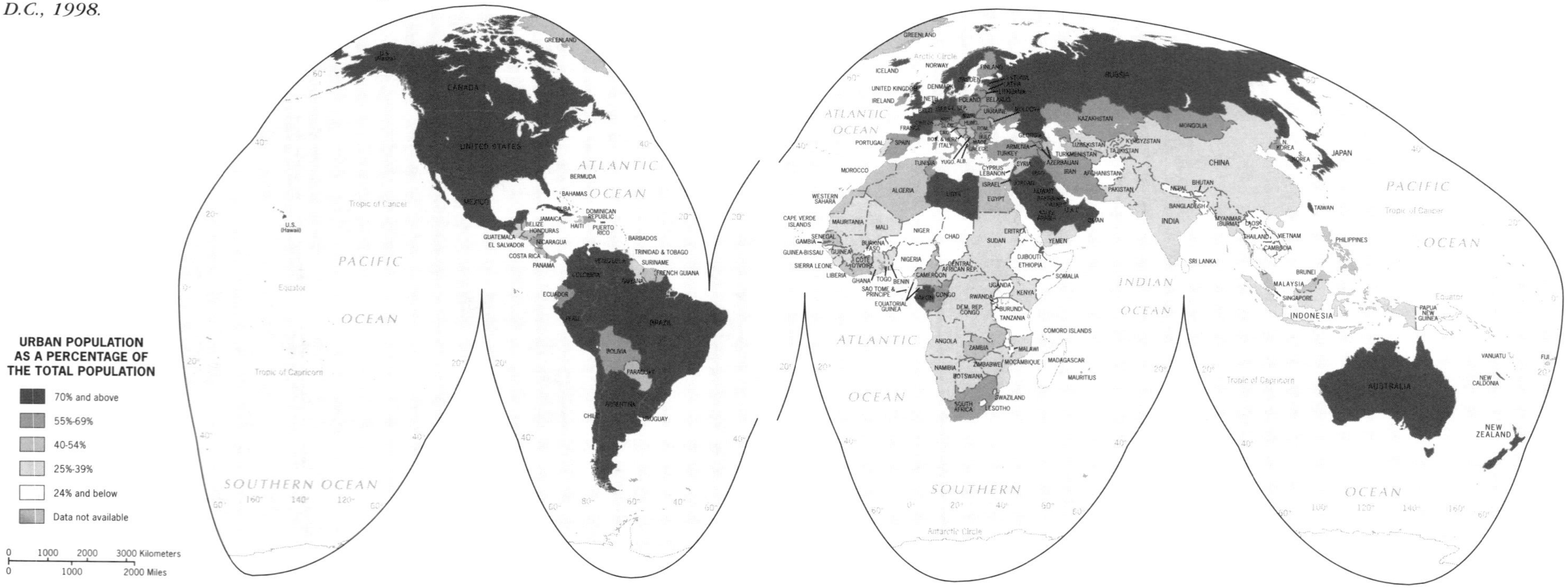

URBAN POPULATION
AS A PERCENTAGE OF
THE TOTAL POPULATION

70% and above
55%-69%
40-54%
25%-39%
24% and below
Data not available

0   1000   2000   3000 Kilometers
0   1000   2000 Miles

136

Figure 18-7 World Metropolitan Area Population. Based on data from numerous, often contradictory, sources, data on urban centers often are inconsistent. *Source: From United Nations, U.S. Census Bureau, Encyclopaedia Britannica Yearbooks, World Bank, Statesman's Yearbook, and other sources.*

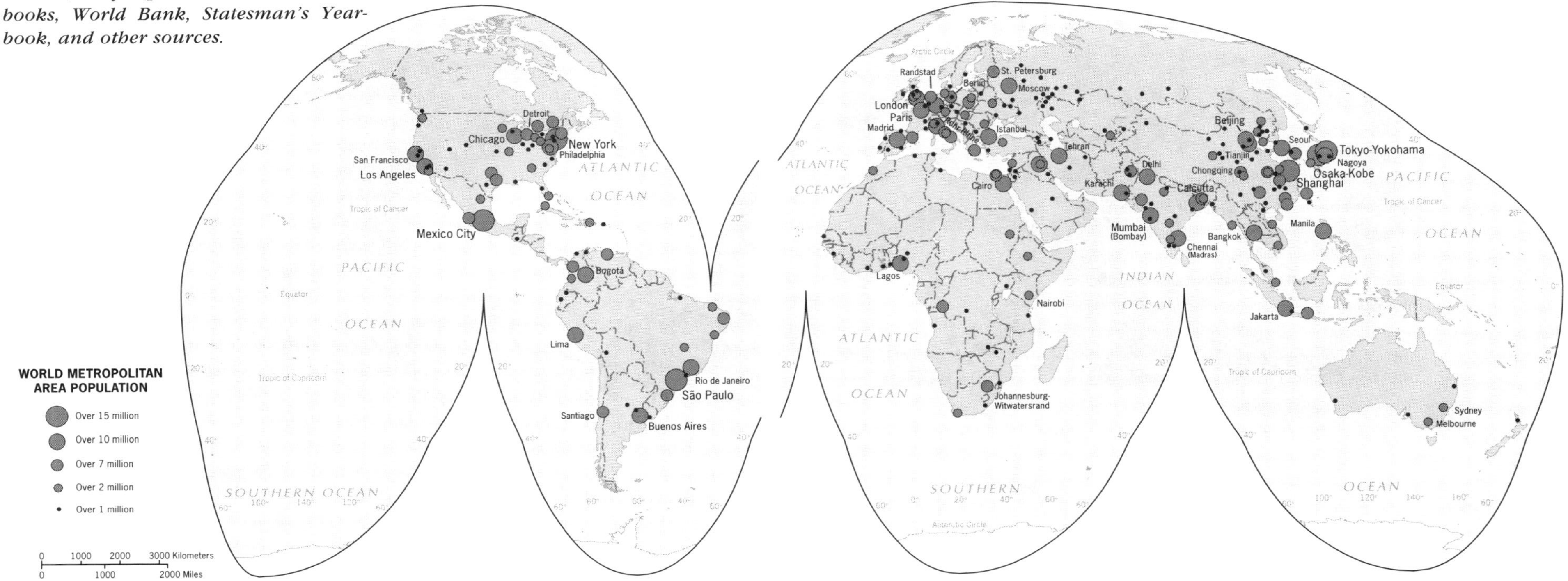

WORLD METROPOLITAN AREA POPULATION
- Over 15 million
- Over 10 million
- Over 7 million
- Over 2 million
- Over 1 million

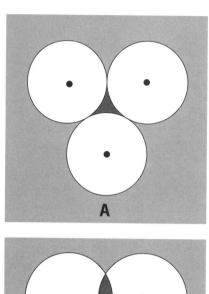

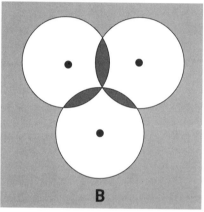

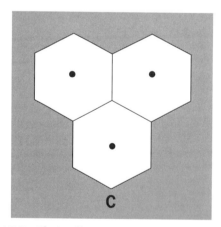

Figure 19-2 Christaller's Hexagonal Trade Areas Surrounding Urban Centers. Constructing Christaller's hexagonal trade areas surrounding urban centers involves: (A) unserved areas shown in purple; (B) purple areas indicate places where the conditions of monopoly would not be fulfilled; and (C) hexagons completely fill an area without overlap.

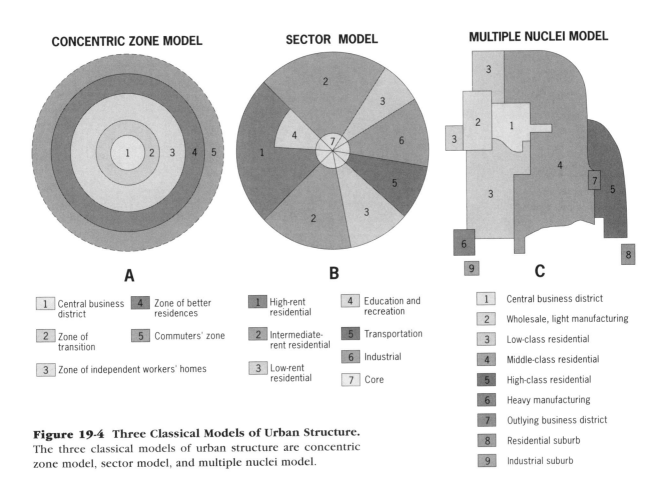

CONCENTRIC ZONE MODEL

A

1 Central business district
2 Zone of transition
3 Zone of independent workers' homes
4 Zone of better residences
5 Commuters' zone

SECTOR MODEL

B

1 High-rent residential
2 Intermediate-rent residential
3 Low-rent residential
4 Education and recreation
5 Transportation
6 Industrial
7 Core

MULTIPLE NUCLEI MODEL

C

1 Central business district
2 Wholesale, light manufacturing
3 Low-class residential
4 Middle-class residential
5 High-class residential
6 Heavy manufacturing
7 Outlying business district
8 Residential suburb
9 Industrial suburb

Figure 19-4 Three Classical Models of Urban Structure.
The three classical models of urban structure are concentric zone model, sector model, and multiple nuclei model.

URBAN REALMS MODEL

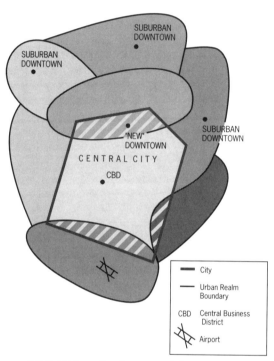

Figure 19-5 Urban Realms Model. The Urban Realms Model includes central business district, central city, new downtown, and suburban downtown. *Source: From T. Hartshorn and P. O. Muller, "Suburban Downtowns and the Transformation of Metropolitan Atlanta's Business Landscape,"* Urban Geography 10 (1989), p. 375. *Reproduced by permission of* Urban Geography.

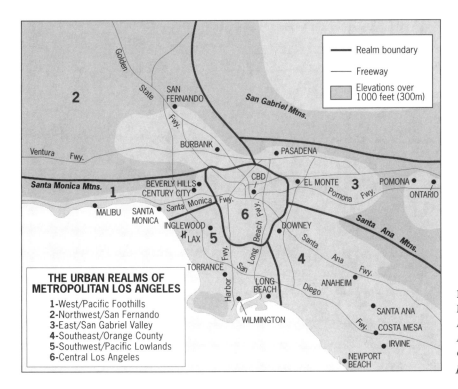

THE URBAN REALMS OF METROPOLITAN LOS ANGELES
1-West/Pacific Foothills
2-Northwest/San Fernando
3-East/San Gabriel Valley
4-Southeast/Orange County
5-Southwest/Pacific Lowlands
6-Central Los Angeles

Figure 19-6 **The Urban Realms of Metropolitan Los Angeles.** *Source: From a map in H. J. de Blij and P. O. Muller,* Geography: Regions and Concepts, *5th ed. New York: Wiley, 1988, p. 220, designed by P. O. Muller.*

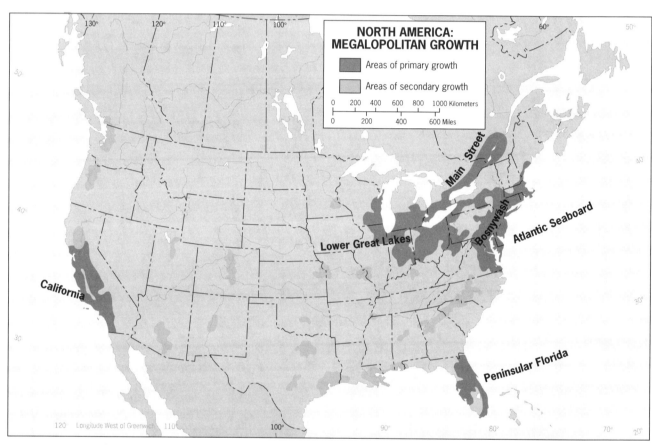

Figure 20-1 North American Megalopolitan Growth. This map shows evolving megalopolises in North America. *Source: From a map in H. J. de Blij and P. O. Muller, Geography: Realms, Regions, and Concepts, 7th ed. New York: Wiley, 1994.*

A NEW AND IMPROVED MODEL
OF LATIN AMERICAN CITY STRUCTURE

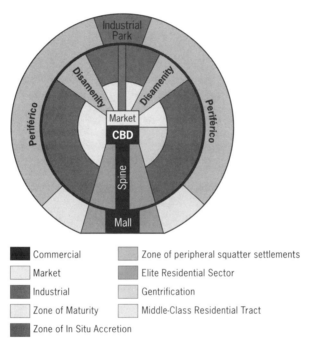

Commercial

Market

Industrial

Zone of Maturity

Zone of In Situ Accretion

Zone of peripheral squatter settlements

Elite Residential Sector

Gentrification

Middle-Class Residential Tract

Figure 20-3 A Generalized Model of Latin American City Structure. This model includes commercial/industrial zones, elite residential sector, zone of maturity, zone of *in situ* accretion, and zone of peripheral squatter settlements. *Source: From E. Griffin and L. Ford, "A Model of Latin American City Structure,"* The Geographical Review *70 (1980), p. 406.*

A GENERALIZED MODEL OF
LAND USE AREAS IN THE LARGE
SOUTHEAST ASIAN CITY

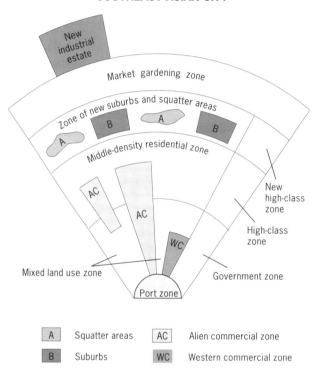

A	Squatter areas	AC	Alien commercial zone
B	Suburbs	WC	Western commercial zone

Figure 20-4 A Generalized Model of Land Use Areas in the Large Southeast Asian City. A model of land use in the large Southeast Asian city includes port zone, government zone, mixed land use zone, high-class zone, new high-class zone, middle-density residential zone, zone of new suburbs and squatter areas, market gardening zone, and new industrial zone. *Source: From T. G. McGee*, The Southeast Asian City, *London: Bell, 1967, p. 128. Reprinted by permission of the publisher.*

THE MODEL AFRICAN CITY

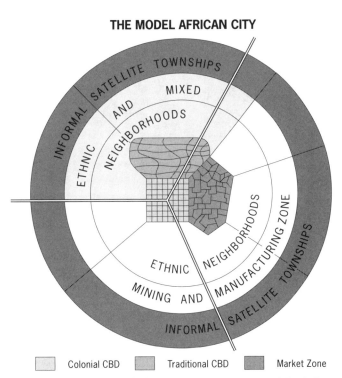

Colonial CBD　Traditional CBD　Market Zone

Figure 20-5 A Model African City. One model of the African city includes colonial CBD, traditional CBD, and market zone.

　　145

Figure 21-1 World Economies.
Source: Based on data from the World Bank, World Development Report 1994. Oxford: Oxford University Press, 1994, pp. 238–239.

WORLD ECONOMIES

- High income economies
- Upper-middle income economies
- Lower-middle income economies
- Low income economies
- Data unavailable

146

Figure 24-1 Increases in Value of Manufacturing Exports to OECD Countries. This map shows the percentage of increases in value of manufacturing exports to OECD countries from major low- and middle-income trading partners, 1970–1992. *Source: The World Bank World Development Report 1994. Infrastructure for Development, Oxford: Oxford University Press.*

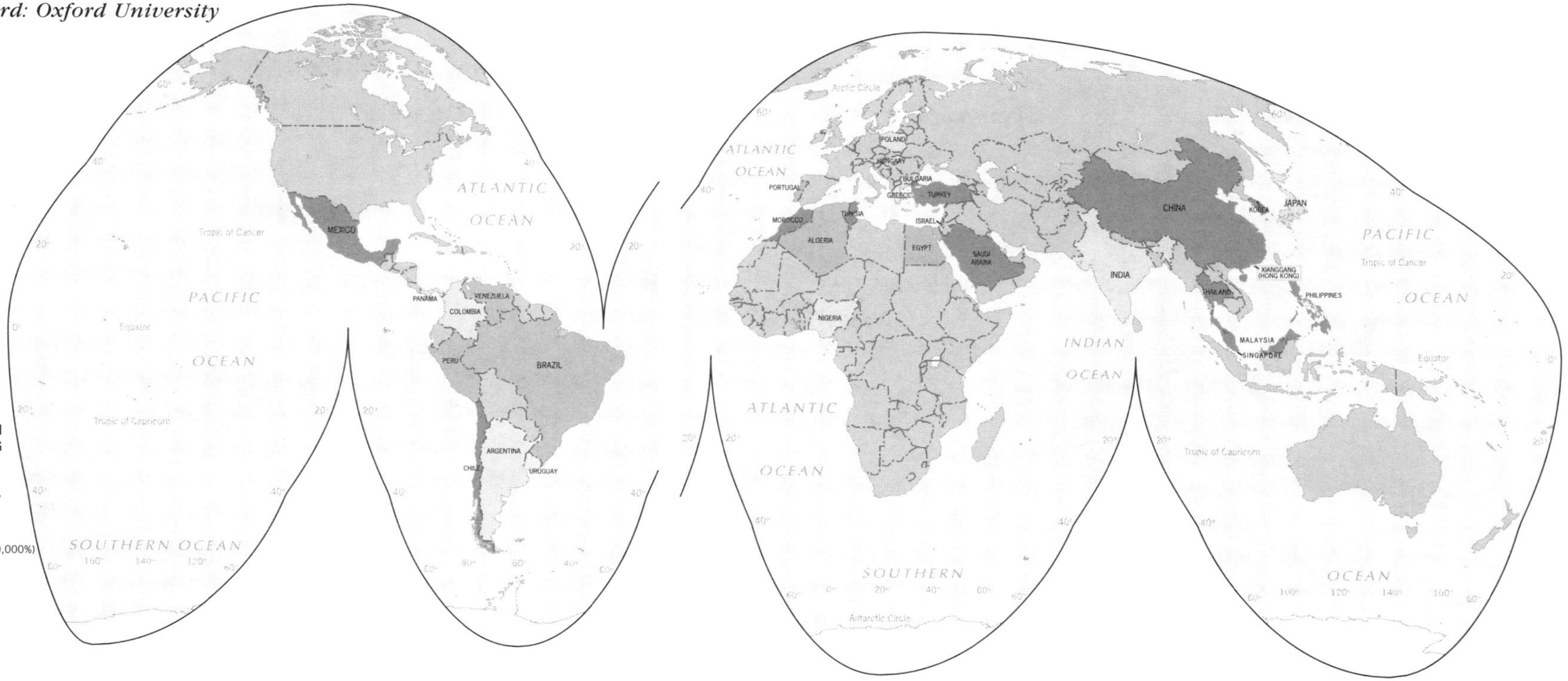

PERCENTAGE INCREASES IN VALUE OF MANUFACTURING EXPORTS TO OECD

Percentage increases in value of manufacturing exports to OECD countries, 1970-1992, from major low and middle-income trading partners.

5001% and above (highest: 40,000%)

2801%-5000%

1000%-2800%

151

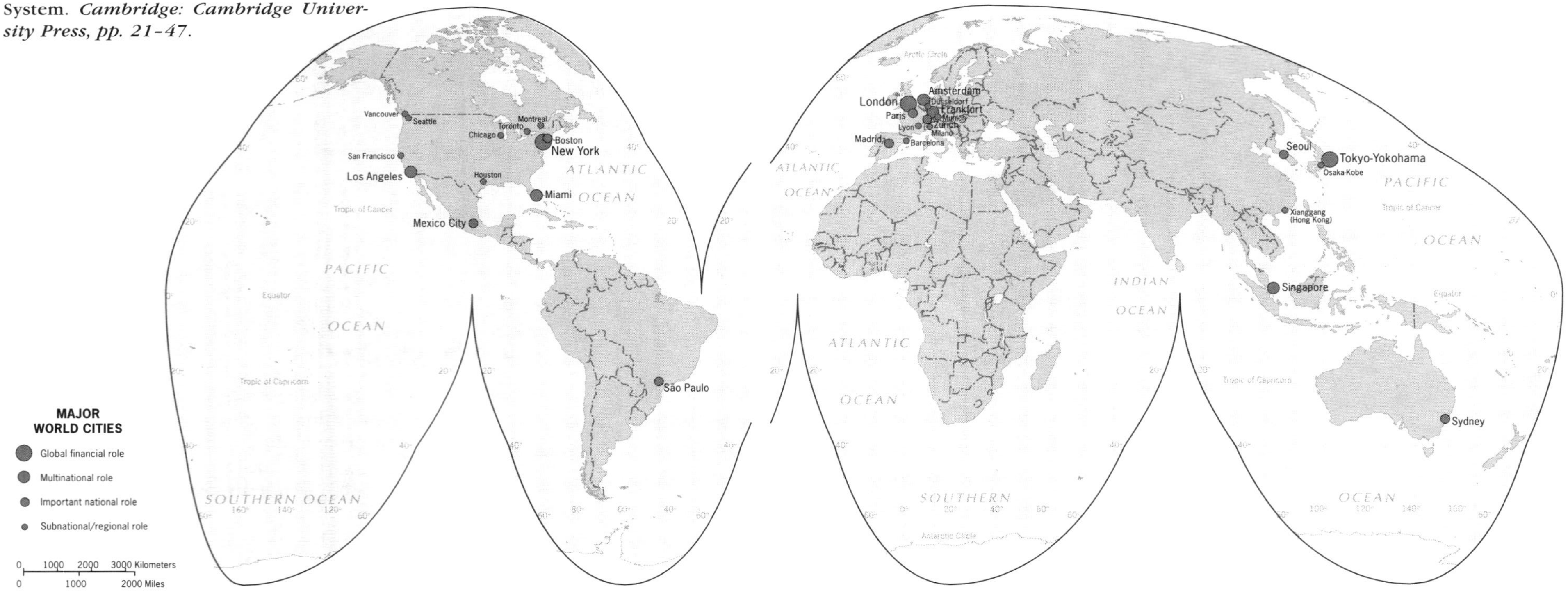
Vancouver
Seattle
San Francisco
Los Angeles
Chicago
Toronto
Montreal
Boston
New York
Houston
Miami
Mexico City
São Paulo
London
Amsterdam
Düsseldorf
Frankfurt
Paris
Lyon
Munich
Zurich
Milano
Madrid
Barcelona
Seoul
Tokyo-Yokohama
Osaka-Kobe
Xianggang (Hong Kong)
Singapore
Sydney
PACIFIC OCEAN
ATLANTIC OCEAN
INDIAN OCEAN
SOUTHERN OCEAN
Equator
Tropic of Cancer
Tropic of Capricorn
Arctic Circle
Antarctic Circle
MAJOR WORLD CITIES
Global financial role
Multinational role
Important national role
Subnational/regional role
0 1000 2000 3000 Kilometers
0 1000 2000 Miles

Figure 24-3 Major World Cities. In 1995 John Friedman delineated the major world cities according to global financial, multinational, national, subnational/regional articulations. *Source: J. Friedman, "Where We Stand in a Decade of World City Research," in P. C. Knox and P. J. Taylor, eds.,* World Cities in a World System. *Cambridge: Cambridge University Press, pp. 21–47.*

Figure 24-4 Access to the Internet.
This map depicts Internet connected computers per 1000 population as of January 1997. *Source: "Access to the Internet," Scientific American 277(1): July 1997, p. 26.*

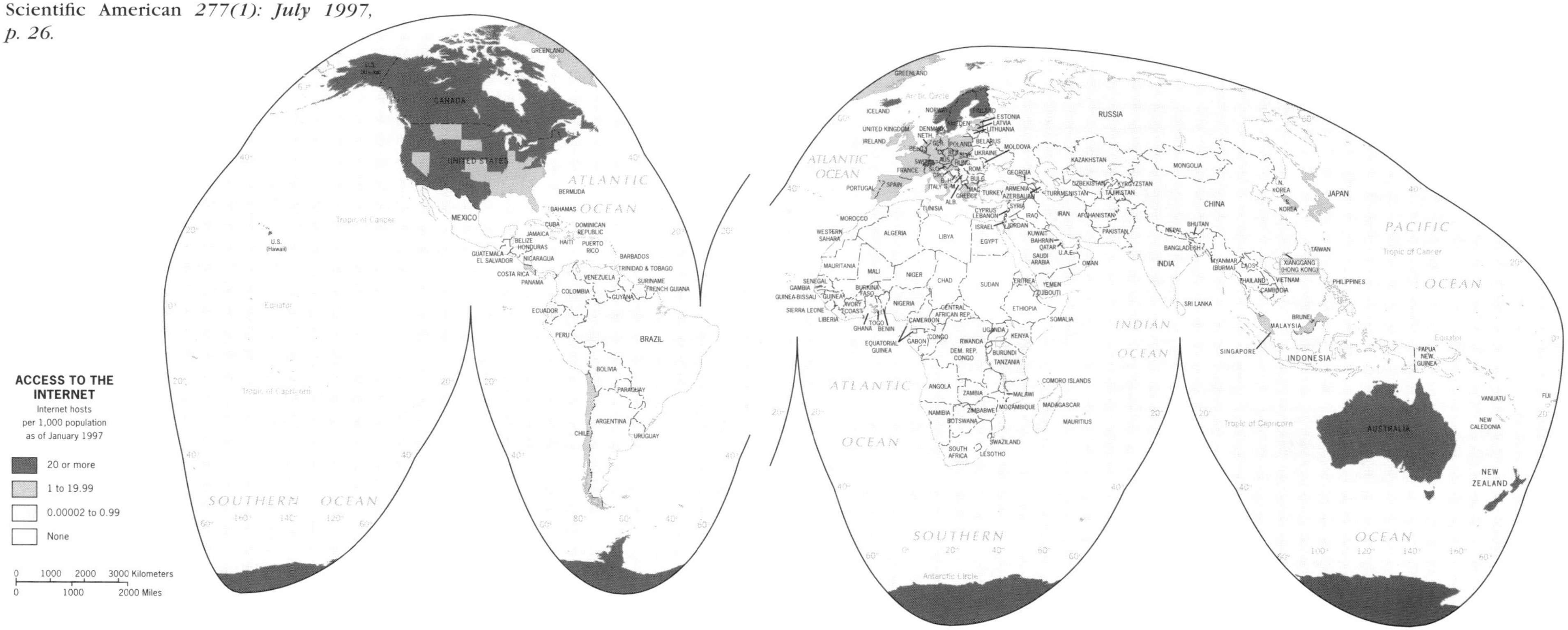

ACCESS TO THE INTERNET
Internet hosts
per 1,000 population
as of January 1997

- 20 or more
- 1 to 19.99
- 0.00002 to 0.99
- None

0   1000   2000   3000 Kilometers
0   1000   2000 Miles

Figure 25-1 States of the World 1999.
The political-geographical fragmentation of the world, 1999, is illustrated on this map. Only the smallest (micro-) states are not shown.

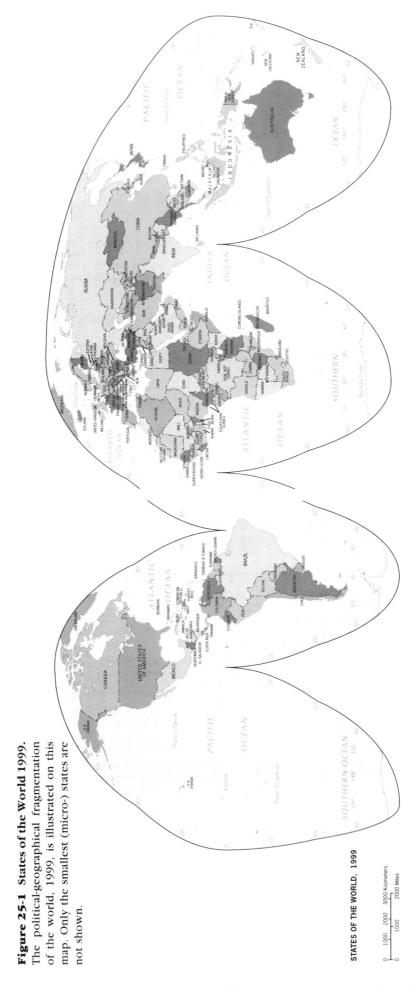

STATES OF THE WORLD, 1999

0 1000 2000 3000 Kilometers
0   1000   2000 Miles

154

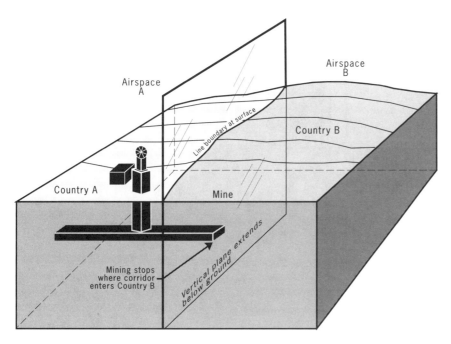

Airspace
A

Airspace
B

Line boundary at surface

Country B

Country A

Mine

Mining stops
where corridor
enters Country B

Vertical plane extends
below ground

Figure 25-4 Political Boundaries on a Vertical Plane. A political boundary is a vertical plane, not merely a line on the ground.

GENETIC POLITICAL BOUNDARY TYPES

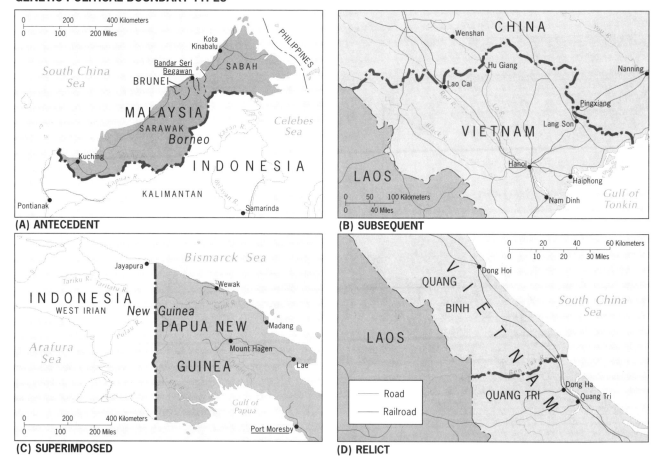

Figure 25-6 Genetic Political Boundary Types. Genetic political boundary types are (A) antecedent, (B) subsequent, (C) superimposed, and (D) relict. *Source: From a map in H. J. de Blij and P. O. Muller*, Realms, Regions, and Concepts, *7th ed. New York: Wiley, 1994.*

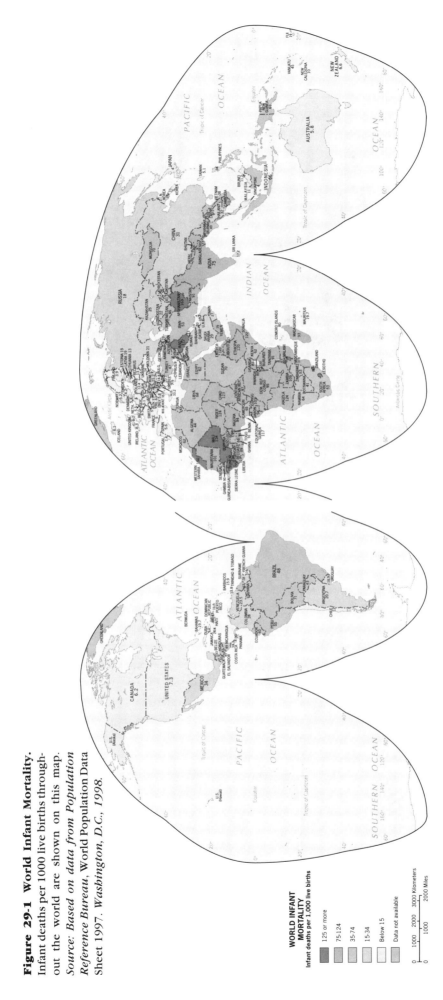

Figure 29-1 World Infant Mortality. Infant deaths per 1000 live births throughout the world are shown on this map. *Source: Based on data from Population Reference Bureau, World Population Data Sheet 1997. Washington, D.C., 1998.*

WORLD INFANT MORTALITY
Infant deaths per 1,000 live births

- 125 or more
- 75–124
- 35–74
- 15–34
- Below 15
- Data not available

0   1000   2000   3000 Kilometers
0   1000   2000 Miles

Figure 29-2 Life Expectancy at Birth.

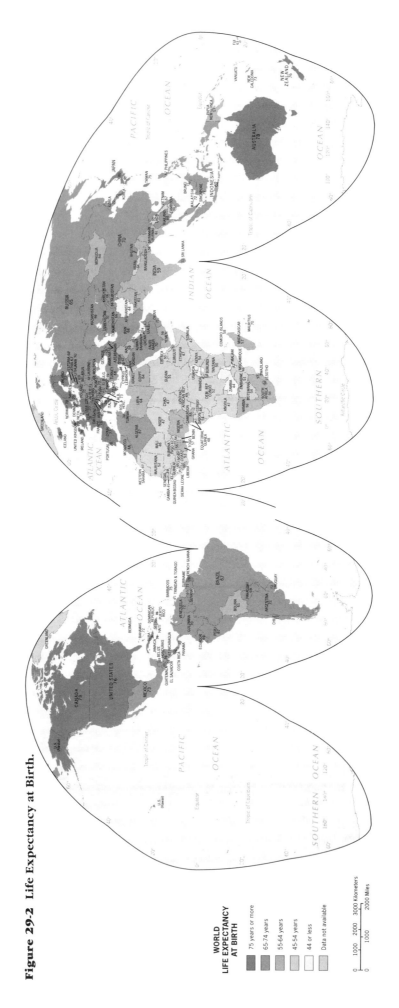

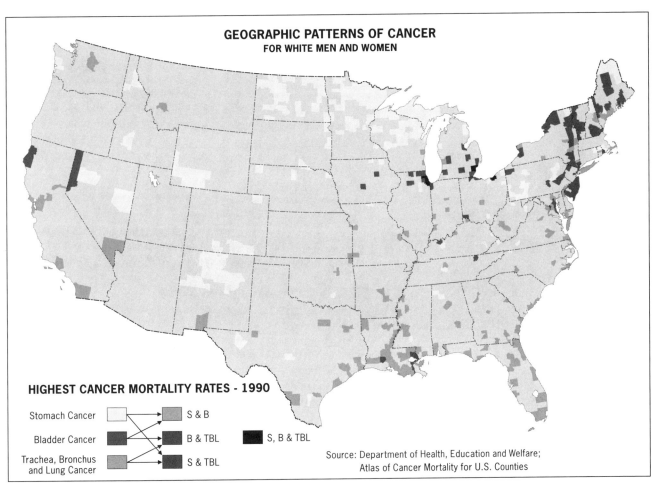

Figure 29-14 Highest Cancer Mortality Rates, 1990. The regional aspects of cancer incidence in the United States as of 1990 are illustrated in this map. *Source: Department of Health, Education and Welfare;* Atlas of Cancer Mortality for U.S. Counties.

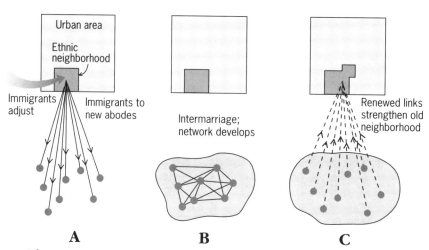

Figure 30-3 Immigration, Intermarriage, and Cultural Revival.

Figure 30-4 Canada's Provinces and Territories. Canada's provinces and territories and their capitals are illustrated here. The entity entitled Nunavut was proposed in 1992 to recognize the territorial rights of indigenous peoples in this area; it formally comes into being in 1999.

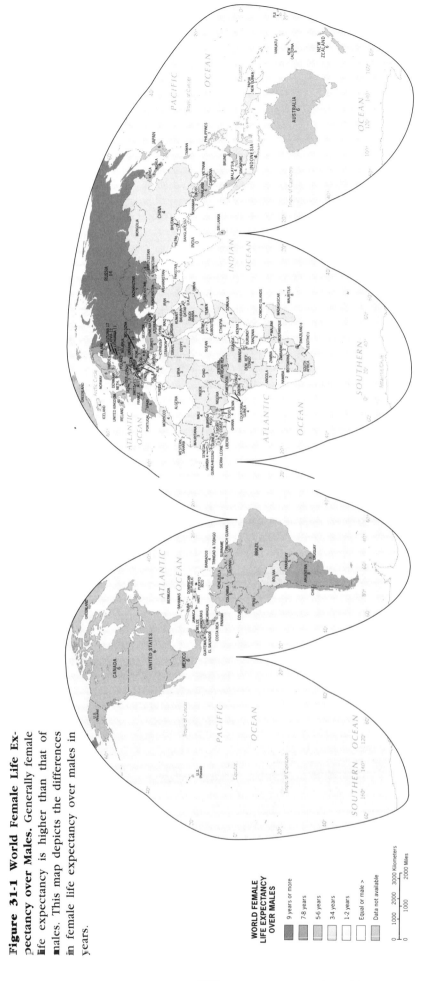

Figure 31-1 World Female Life Expectancy over Males. Generally female life expectancy is higher than that of males. This map depicts the differences in female life expectancy over males in years.

WORLD FEMALE LIFE EXPECTANCY OVER MALES

- 9 years or more
- 7-8 years
- 5-6 years
- 3-4 years
- 1-2 years
- Equal or male >
- Data not available

1000   2000   3000 Kilometers
0
0   1000   2000 Miles

166

Figure 31-2 World Maternal Mortality Rate. Maternal mortality rate reflects the number of deaths per 100,000 live births. This map shows the maternal mortality rate throughout the world. *Source: Data from United Nations, The World's Women 1970–1990. New York: United Nations, 1991, p. 67.*

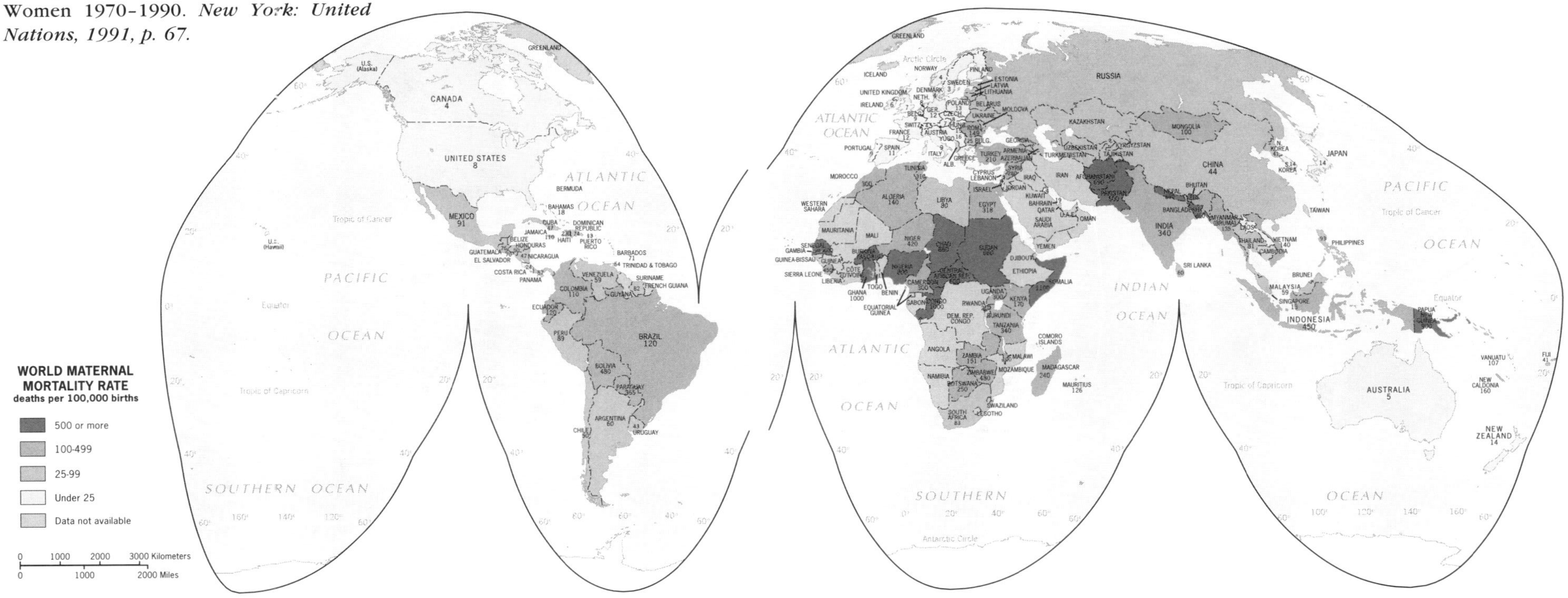

WORLD MATERNAL MORTALITY RATE
deaths per 100,000 births

- 500 or more
- 100-499
- 25-99
- Under 25
- Data not available

0   1000   2000   3000 Kilometers
0   1000   2000 Miles

167

Figure 31-3 Women's Education as a Ratio of Men's. This map represents the average of data for all three levels of education during 1985–1987. *Source: Data from United Nations. The World's Women 1970–1990. New York: United Nations, 1991, p. 50. Later informal data suggest that the situation has been deteriorating since the late 1980s.*

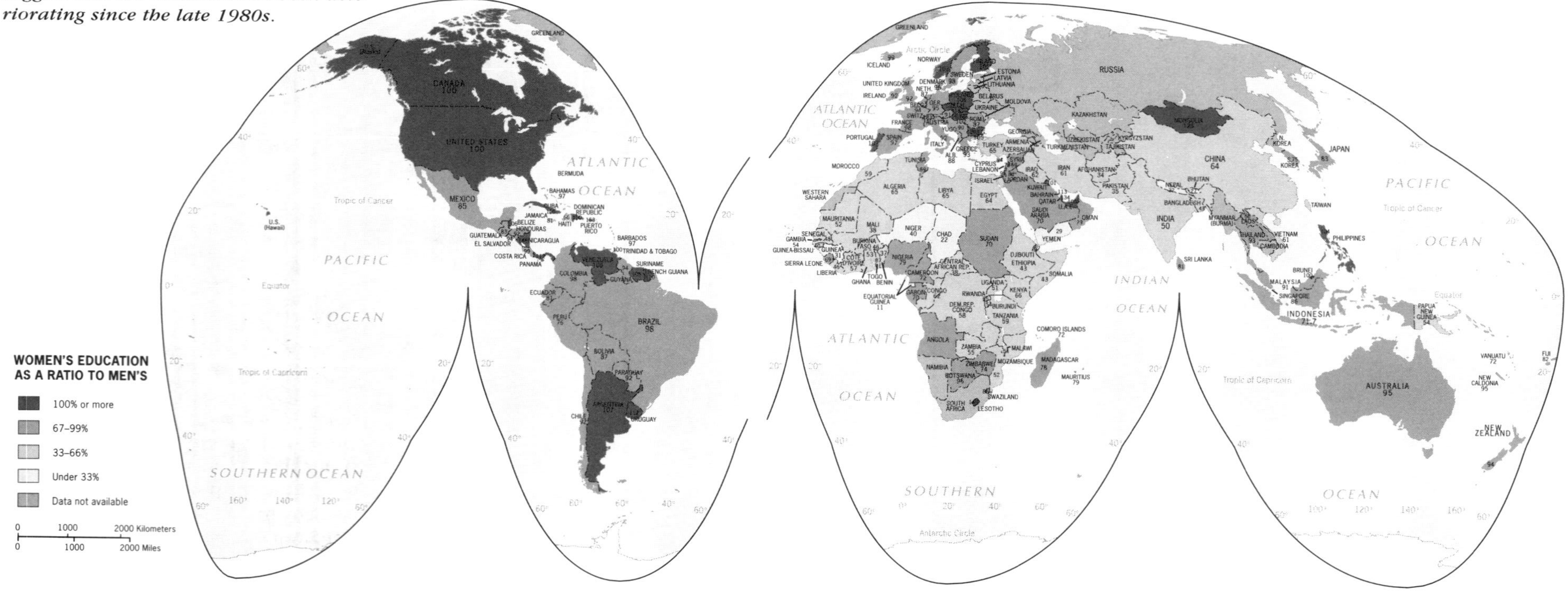

WOMEN'S EDUCATION
AS A RATIO TO MEN'S

- 100% or more
- 67–99%
- 33–66%
- Under 33%
- Data not available

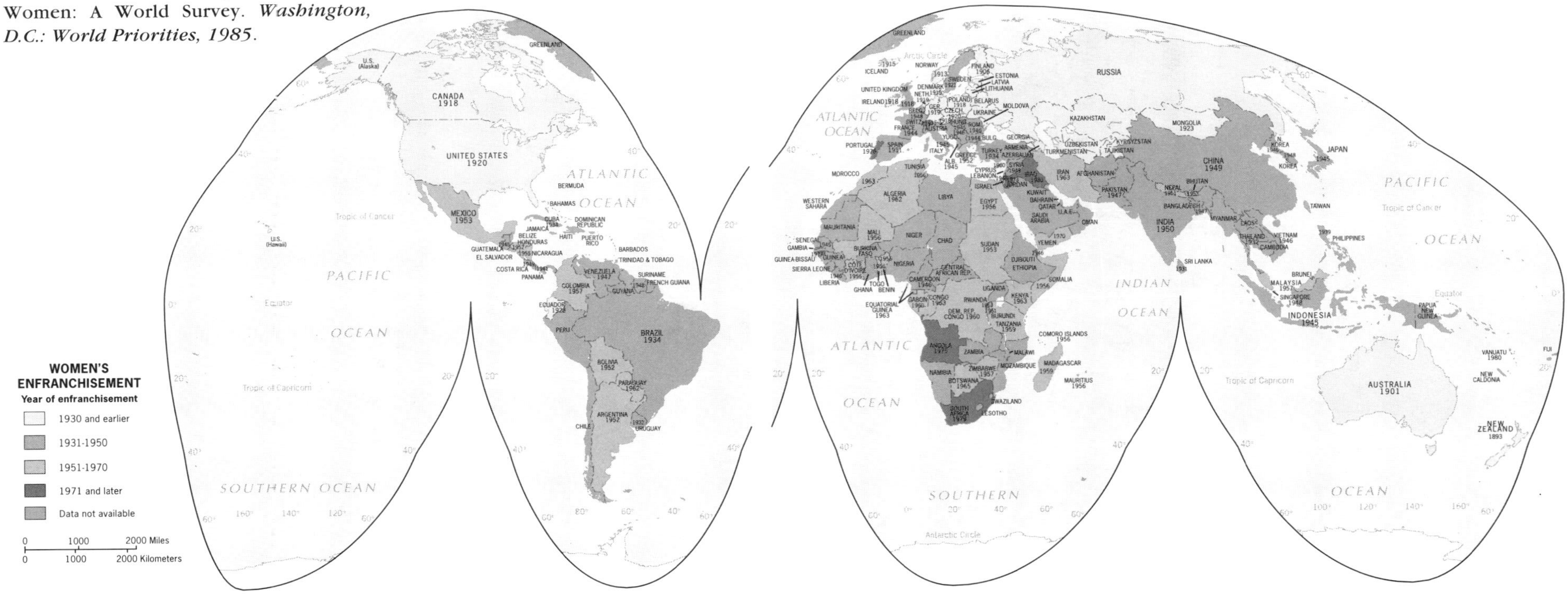

Figure 31-4 Women's Enfranchisement. The years that women were enfranchised are shown on this world map. *Source: Data from United Nations, The World's Women 1970–1990. New York: United Nations, 1991, p. 39 and from other sources including R. L. Sivard, Women: A World Survey. Washington, D.C.: World Priorities, 1985.*

WOMEN'S ENFRANCHISEMENT
Year of enfranchisement

- 1930 and earlier
- 1931-1950
- 1951-1970
- 1971 and later
- Data not available

0   1000   2000 Miles
0   1000   2000 Kilometers

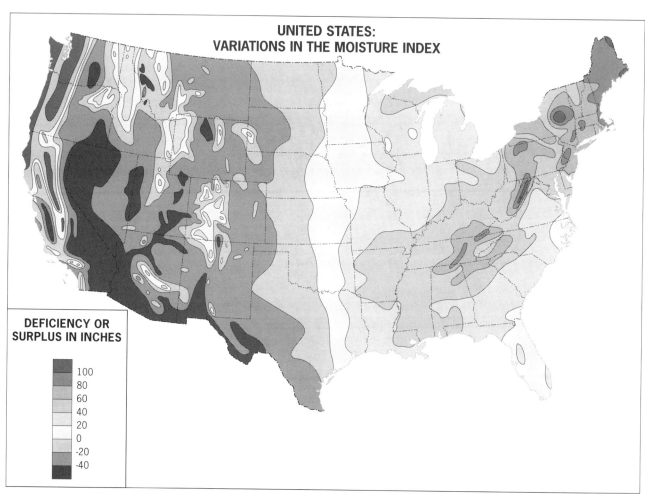

Figure 32-2 Variations in the Moisture Index in the United States. This map shows the variation in moisture surplus and deficiency in the United States. *Source: From a map in E. A. Fernald and D. J. Patton, editors,* Water Resources Atlas of Florida *(Tallahassee: Florida State University, 1984) p. 6.*

Figure 35-1 Devolutionary Pressures in Europe. Centrifugal forces have resulted in devolutionary pressures in various places in Europe. *Source: From a map in H. J. de Blij and P. O. Muller*, Geography: Realms, Regions, and Concepts, 8th ed. *(New York: Wiley, 1997).*

175

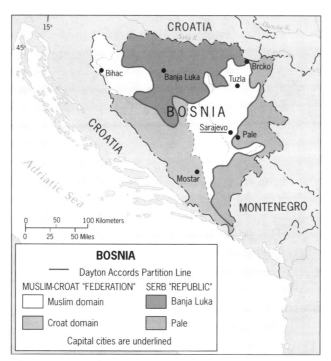

Figure 35-2 The Partition of Bosnia. The Dayton Accords Partition Line separates Serb from non-Serb entities. *Source: From a map in H. J. de Blij and P. O. Muller,* Geography: Realms, Regions, and Concepts, *8th ed. Revised (New York: Wiley, 1998).*

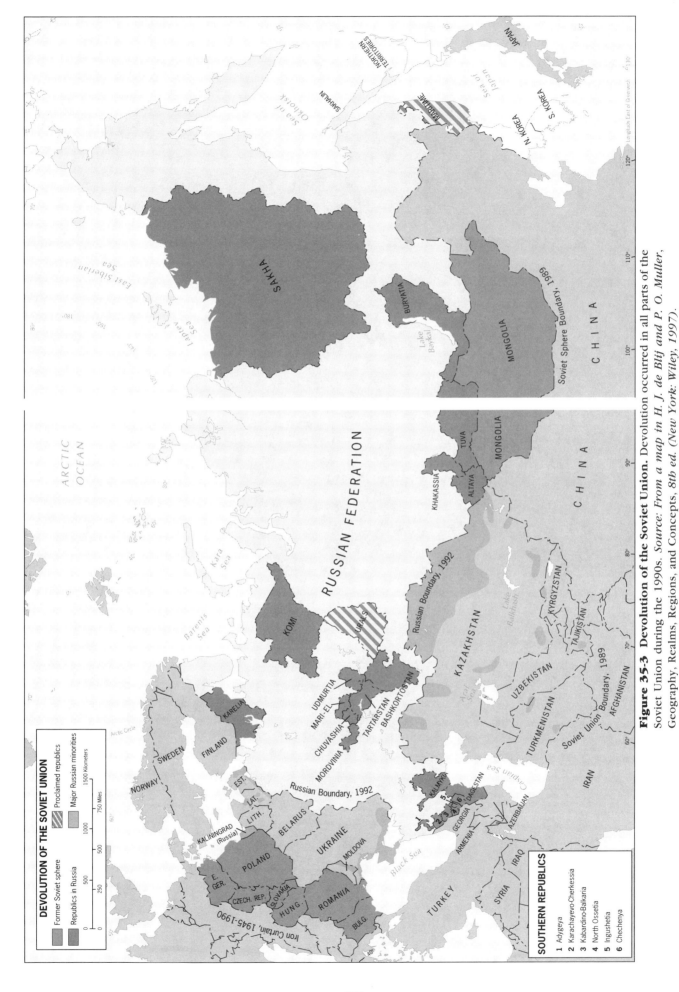

Figure 35-3 Devolution of the Soviet Union. Devolution occurred in all parts of the Soviet Union during the 1990s. *Source: From a map in H. J. de Blij and P. O. Muller, Geography, Realms, Regions, and Concepts, 8th ed. (New York: Wiley, 1997).*

DEVOLUTION OF THE SOVIET UNION

- Former Soviet sphere
- Republics in Russia
- Proclaimed republics
- Major Russian minorities

SOUTHERN REPUBLICS

1 Adygeya
2 Karachayevo-Cherkessia
3 Kabardino-Balkaria
4 North Ossetia
5 Ingushetia
6 Chechenya

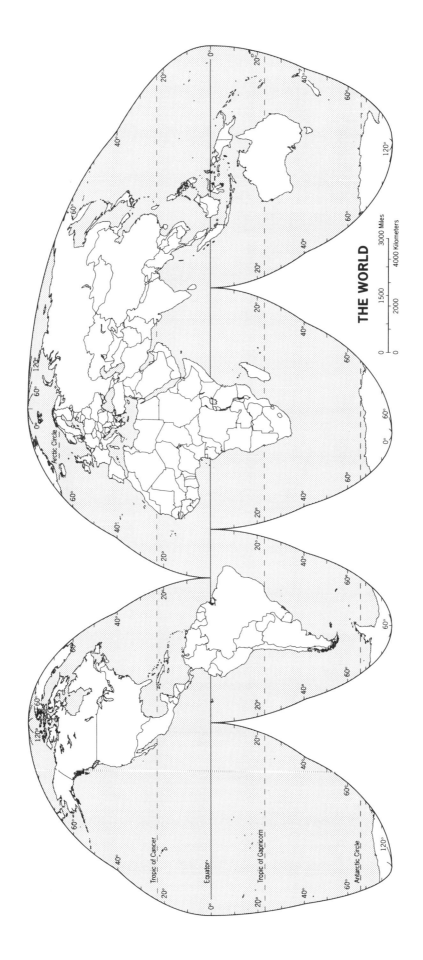

THE WORLD

3000 Miles
4000 Kilometers

0   1500   3000
0   2000   4000

Arctic Circle

Tropic of Cancer

Equator

Tropic of Capricorn

Antarctic Circle

EUROPE

0   200   400   600 Kilometers
0   100   200   300 Miles

Arctic Circle

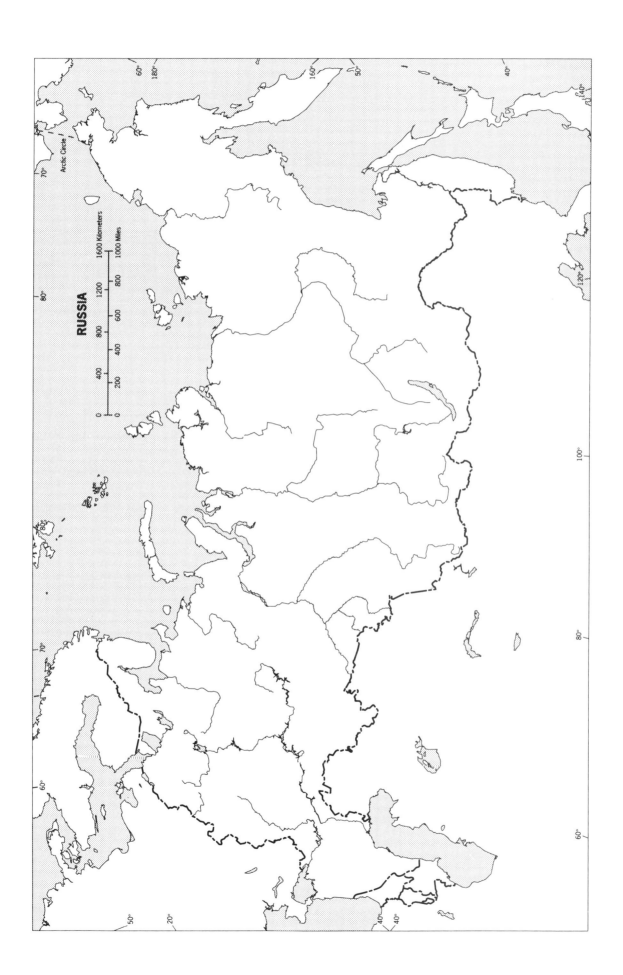

RUSSIA

Arctic Circle

1600 Kilometers
1000 Miles

181

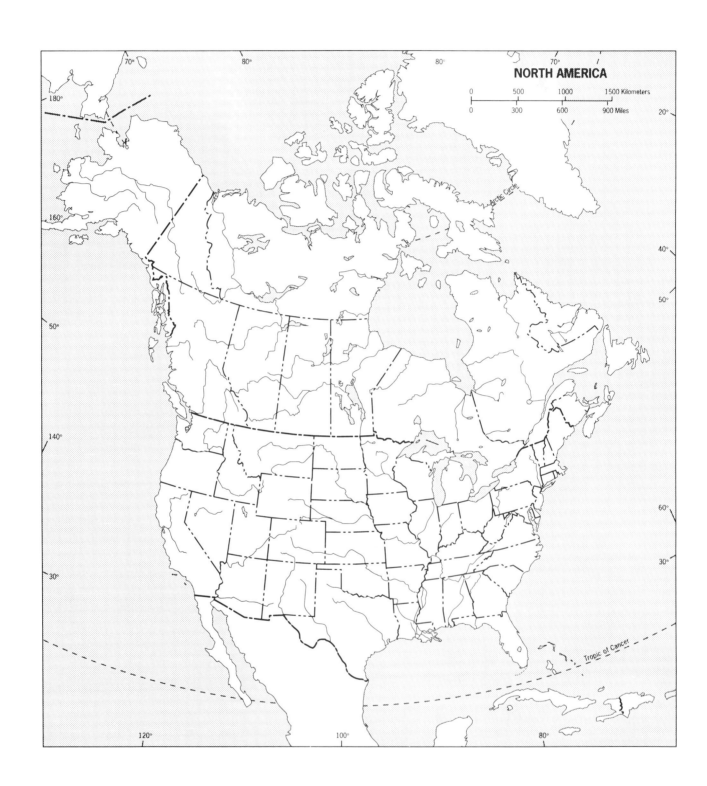

NORTH AMERICA

Arctic Circle

Tropic of Cancer

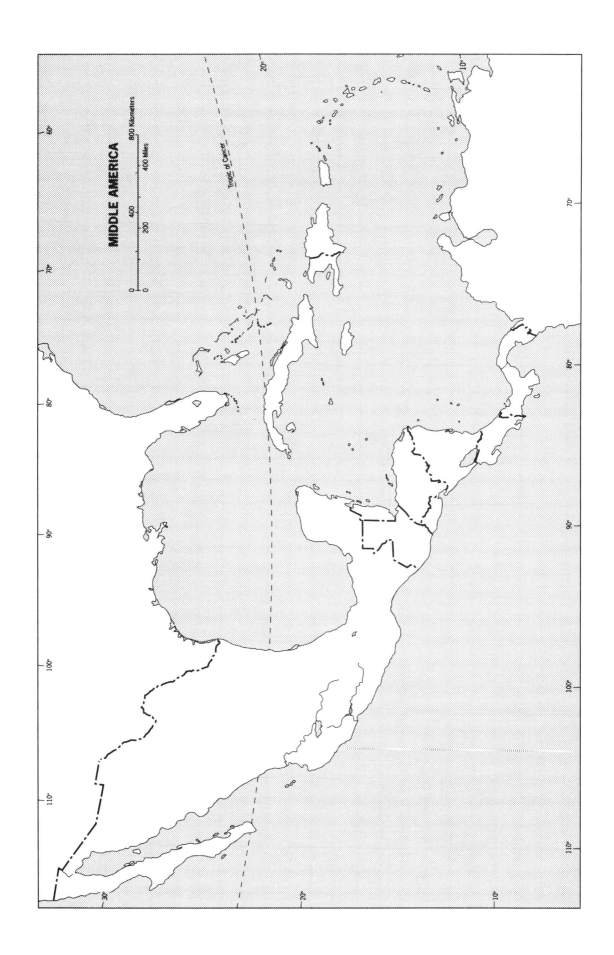

MIDDLE AMERICA

Tropic of Cancer

800 Kilometers
400 Miles

183

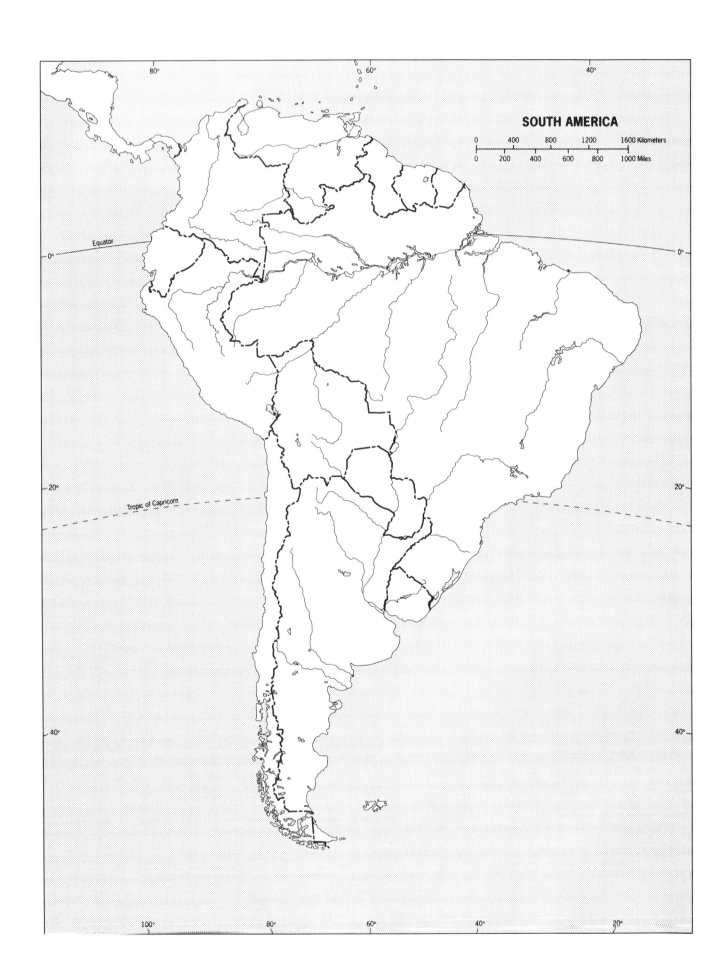

SOUTH AMERICA

| 0 | 400 | 800 | 1200 | 1600 Kilometers |
| 0 | 200 | 400 | 600 | 800 | 1000 Miles |

Equator

0°

20°

Tropic of Capricorn

40°

80°

60°

40°

100°

80°

60°

40°

20°

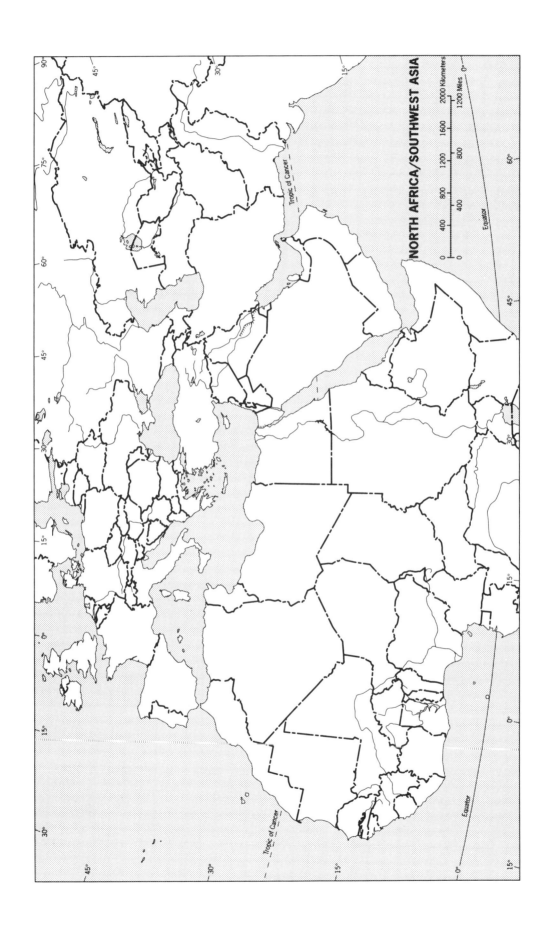

NORTH AFRICA/SOUTHWEST ASIA

185

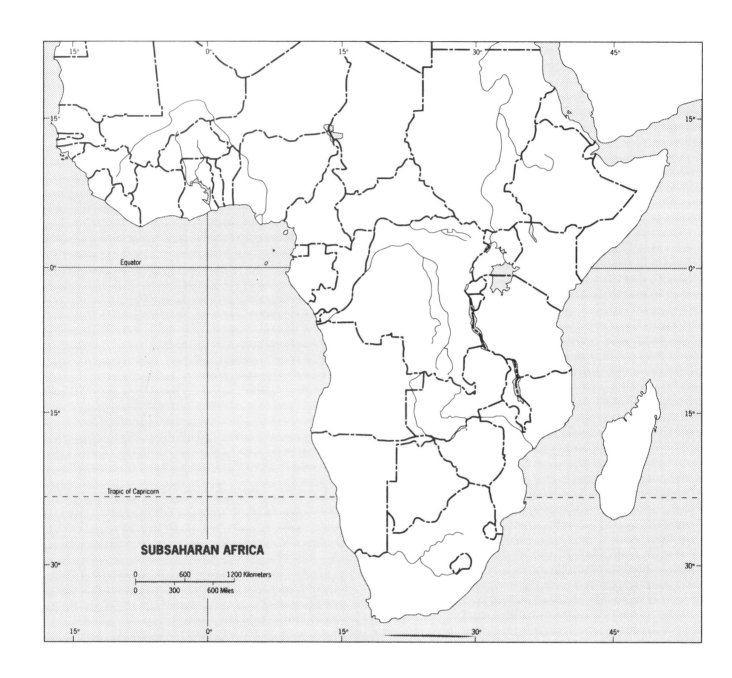

SUBSAHARAN AFRICA

Equator

Tropic of Capricorn

0   600   1200 Kilometers
0   300   600 Miles

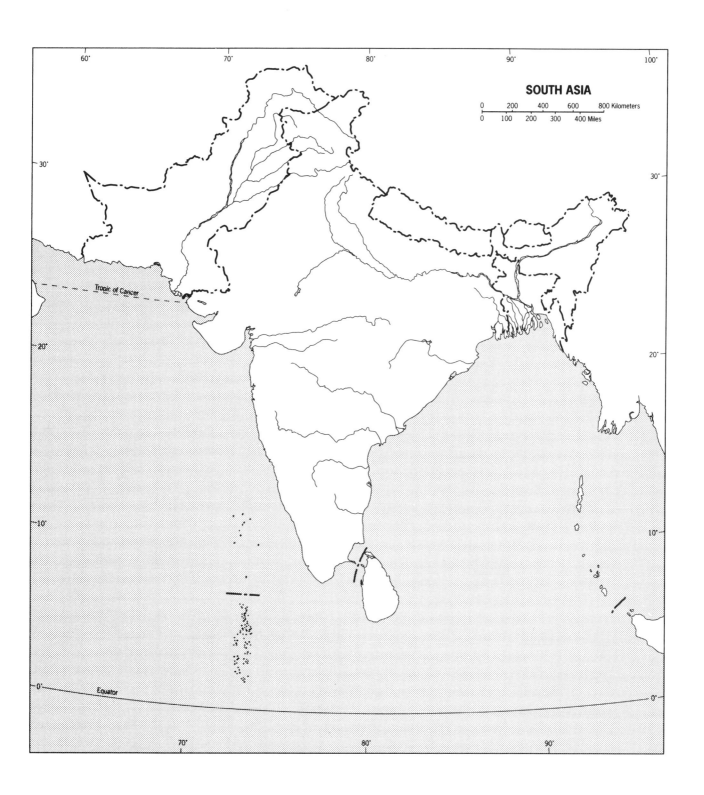

SOUTH ASIA

0	200	400	600	800 Kilometers
0	100 200	300	400 Miles	

Tropic of Cancer

Equator

187

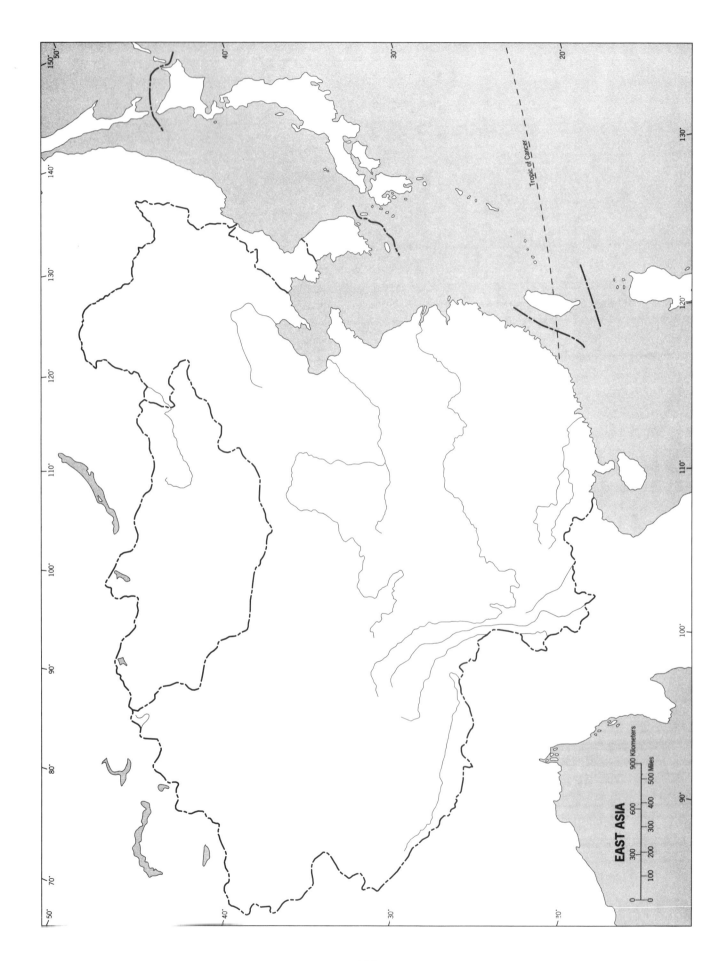

EAST ASIA

900 Kilometers

500 Miles

Tropic of Cancer

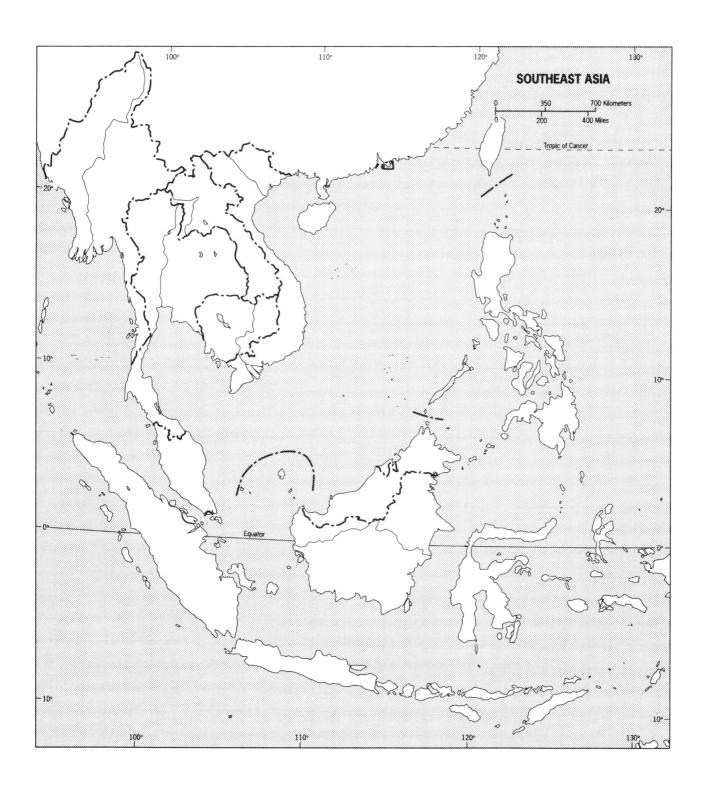

SOUTHEAST ASIA

0   350   700 Kilometers
0   200   400 Miles

Tropic of Cancer

Equator

189

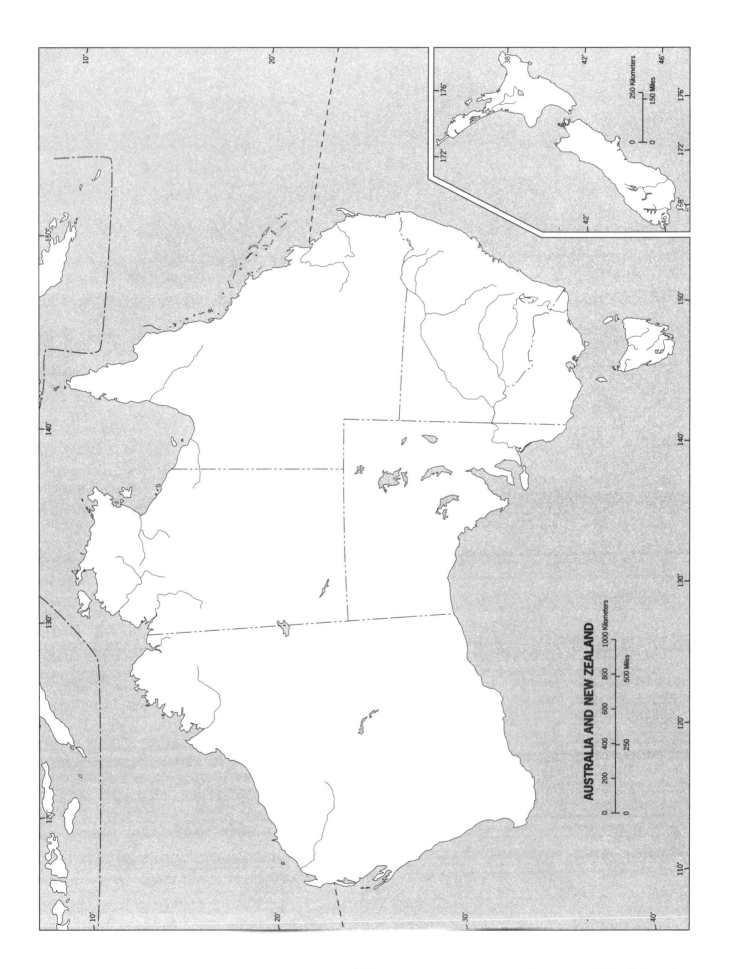

AUSTRALIA AND NEW ZEALAND

VIRTUAL FIELD GUIDE

PART ONE
GEOGRAPHY, CULTURE, AND ENVIRONMENT

GOALS: To understand the nature of geography as the science of location and a core discipline that serves as a "bridge" between the social sciences and the physical sciences. With this, you, as a participant in the activity, will discern that the focus of geography is not so much the study of certain content material, as much as it is the spatial perspective of examining phenomena on our planet. You will appreciate the two-way interaction between humans and their environment. In view of the educational reforms taking place at the state and national levels, you will acquire an understanding about how an increased awareness of geography will help to develop a more responsible and enlightened citizenry that can solve both local and global spatial problems.

ACTIVITIES: Constructing hometown geographies, debating cultural imperialism, tracing the diffusion of rock & roll, and playing roles in a discussion of acid rain.

ACTIVITY 1.1: "Thinking Globally, Acting Locally!"

INTRODUCTION: Many students taking human geography as a college general education requirement have not had a formal geography course, *per se*, since junior high school perhaps. In many schools across the United States, geography got "lost" in the social science shuffle of the 'sixties era. As a result, a fair amount of incoming American college students have the false impression that geography is a "*trivial pursuit*," as their concept of what constitutes geography is shaped largely by the successful board game of that name, or what is listed under the geography category on the popular television show *Jeopardy!* But in 1985, the organization known as *G.E.N.I.P.*, or, the Geographic Education National Implementation Project, was formed to institute, update, and enrich geography programs in grades K-12 in American schools. *G.E.N.I.P.* is a collaboration between the major organizations in the field of geography: the National Council for Geographic Education, the Association of American Geographers, the American Geographical Society, and the National Geographic Society. Read about *G.E.N.I.P.* and the resources it offers at the ***National Council for Geographic Education*** Web site (WWW 1.1).

The *G.E.N.I.P.* collaboration has organized the study of geography around what are popularly referred to as "The Five Fundamental Themes of Geography." The themes are:

1) Location (both specific and relative)
2) Characteristics of a Place (both physical and human)
3) Human/Environment Interaction (a two-way street)
4) Movement
5) Regions (physical, cultural, economic, political; formal and functional)

For an elaboration of these themes, see the ***U.S. Department of Education*** Web site (WWW 1.2). These fundamental themes may be used to study geography at both local and global levels of analyses. A commonly used slogan among geographers is "*Think Globally, Act Locally.*"

Let us begin our study of human geography at the local level. Using the five fundamental geography themes, compose a typed, detailed outline of approximately two pages in length, describing the geography of your hometown, or another familiar place. If you live in a large city, you may choose to describe just your neighborhood within the city. The outline should be organized with the five themes listed as the major outline headings (i.e., Roman numerals). Your three or four subheadings per theme should be a sufficient introduction to the basic geography of the place.

The instructor *may* require that you use this outlining activity to learn basic geographic concepts, or may increase the requirements of this activity and assign it as a "capstone" research paper that integrates what you have learned and researched in your human and cultural geography course throughout the semester.

It would be appropriate to design a map to accompany your outline. The map should include the location of places mentioned within the outline/paper (for example, note in the southeastern corner of the city a water treatment plant that you have possibly mentioned in your outline). To do this part, you could use the *Mapquest Web Site* (WWW 1.3) to locate a street map of the location you will report on.

Focus on the geographic (i.e., spatial) aspects of the place. Minimize the historical, political, and social aspects of your town, unless they are examined for their geographic attributes or connections. You should use some combination of data sources (federal, state, and local government agency documents; regional newspaper articles; chamber of commerce materials; planning agency documents; utility reports; real estate agency data sheets; topographic maps; etc.). Most of these sources can be accessed through the Internet. Many towns and cities now have their own home page. That should be the first place to look for information for this activity. The federal government and state governments will provide additional links to excellent data sources for this assignment. Here is a list to get you started:

> *United States Census Bureau* (WWW 1.4)

> *Federal Agency Statistics* (WWW 1.5)

> *City & County Data Book* (WWW 1.6)

> *United States Geological Survey* (WWW 1.7)

> *Population Reference Bureau* (for state-level environmental data) (WWW 1.8)

> *Massachusetts* (as an example of a state data source) (WWW 1.9)

Here is a guideline with examples for the kinds of information that you may include in your outline and paper:

1. Location:
    a) specific:
             - latitude and longitude of the center of town or town hall
             - the intersection of specific highways
             - the main site feature of the place (e.g., at the confluence of two rivers)
    b) relative:
             - a location half-way between two big cities
             - a location in the southeastern part of your state
             - about an hour's drive from the state capital

2. Characteristics of a Place:
    a) physical
             - climatic classification
             - soil classification
             - landform classification

     b) human:
- population characteristics (age, gender, race, ethnicity, etc.)
- religious affiliations
- languages spoken
- occupations (blue/ white collar; primary, secondary, tertiary, etc.)
- political affiliations (Democrat, Independent, Republican, etc.)

3. Human/Environment Interaction:
     a) water supply and treatment
     b) waste disposal
     c) pollution
     d) hazard preparedness

4. Movement:
     a) transportation modes and routes
     b) physical movements (primary wind direction, ocean currents, etc.)
     c) migrations
     e) diffusion (innovations, beliefs, customs, etc.)

5. Regions:
     a) Physical
- landform
- climate
- geologic plate
     b) Cultural
- ethnic
- religious
- language
     c) Economic
- sectors of the economy
- trade
- major resources
     d) Political
- zoning
- township
- county
- Congressional District
     e) Formal
- Corn Belt
- Manufacturing Belt
- New England
     f) Functional
- watershed
- commuter field

     195

ACTIVITY 1.2: We're # 1! Cultural Imperialism

INTRODUCTION: Cultures can be many things, but they are certainly not static. Cultures can be changed through innovations and inventions, diffusion, acculturation, and revitalization. With the twentieth century advancements in communications, transportation, and trade, cultures in many parts of the world have become increasingly dynamic. Some nations fear an eventual loss of cultural identity with ever-increasing global interconnections. *Cultural imperialism* has been defined as the emerging global culture dominated by the world's superpower, the United States. Some argue that U.S. cultural influence is at least as strong as its military influence. Industrialized nations have responded in various ways to America's cultural dominance. France has become particularly wary of U.S. influence (e.g., *la loi Toubon* of 1994, a law which forbids French public entities and corporations engaged in public activities from using English expressions where there is a French equivalent). Canada has "allowed" considerable American cultural influence (e.g., most of the current National Hockey League franchises are now located in the U.S.). Since World War II, Japan has incorporated whole segments of American culture (e.g., baseball & fast food), yet has remained distinctively Japanese. The less industrialized nations have also had different responses to American cultural dominance. Many of the Islamic-dominated nations of the Middle East have little tolerance for American cultural influences and use censorship and other tactics to keep this influence to a minimum. Some additional cultural conflicts between less developed nations and the U.S. grew out of the Cold War which often pitted "godless communists" versus "corrupt capitalists."

This activity raises several opinion questions. 1) Does U.S. cultural imperialism exist, and, if yes, in what ways? 2) If no, are we simply witnessing the development of a "global" culture that currently happens to be largely influenced by the United States? 3) Or, will increased nationalism maintain separate and distinct cultures, with no one culture being dominant?

> ReseAnne Sims' "The United States vs. the World: A Theoretical Look at Cultural Imperialism," at the site of *The University of Texas* (WWW 1.10).

> Former U.S. Ambassador to Finland, Derek N. Shearer's "Hollywood: It's Not Cultural Imperialism, It's World Culture," see the *U.S. Embassy* Web site (WWW 1.11).

> David Rothkopf's "In Praise of Cultural Imperialism," at the *Mt. Holyoke College Web site* (WWW 1.12).

> Douglas Rushkoff's "Let Them Eat Apple Pie? Cultural Imperialism and the Internet," at the *Arkzin* Web site (WWW 1.13).

> Berlingeri, Brett, & Gokyigit's "Cultural Imperialism," at the *Harvard University* Web site (WWW 1.14).

After you have decided which point of view you wish to support, collect information in the virtual field to support your argument. You then might join like-minded students in one section of the room to work together to strengthen your argument in order to discuss and debate with the individuals and groups taking the other two perspectives.

ACTIVITY 1.3: Rock & Roll Is Here To Stay!

INTRODUCTION: Although the United States has been called a "*melting pot*" because of numerous ethnic influences from its wide range and history of immigration, one aspect of American culture that originated in the United States is that of rock and roll music. The world-wide exposure of this native American musical style is a classic example of cultural diffusion. Simply defined, diffusion is the spreading of ideas and objects by whatever means. Diffusion can occur through direct observation, word of mouth, the written word, or recorded sights and sounds. Human geographers are primarily interested in the spatial aspects of diffusion. Some of the key questions that geographers ask about diffusion of some cultural phenomenon include:

1. Where and when did the idea or item originate?
2. How far did this idea or item spread?
3. How long did it take this idea or item to spread?
4. By what means did it spread?
5. Did anyone or anything slow or prevent its movement?
6. Was this a contiguous or non-contiguous movement?
7. Was the concept or idea altered as it diffused?
8. Which segments of the population accepted this concept or idea?

In this activity, use the Internet to research and respond in short-answer format to the eight short-answer questions posed above, using rock and roll music as the subject in this study of diffusion. The following sites may be used to answer these questions:

Visit the **Rock and Roll Hall of Fame** in Cleveland, Ohio (WWW 1.15).

Refer to the *History of Rock and Roll* (WWW 1.16) Web site.

Travel back half a century to *The Fifties* (WWW 1.17), for information from the rock and roll's early years.

To focus on rock and roll's original artists, see the Web site *Biddeford* (WWW 1.18).

See the Rock & Roll series on the *Public Broadcasting System* (WWW 1.19).

To see how TV impacted this musical style, see the *House of Music* (WWW 1.20).

ACTIVITY 1.4: Rain Of Terror

INTRODUCTION: The interaction between humans and their environment is one of the five fundamental themes of geography. This interaction is a two-way street. Greater numbers of humans than ever before are exposed to deadly natural hazards (e.g., earthquakes, hurricanes, tornadoes, etc.). With the world's population at approximately six billion inhabitants, the negative impacts caused by increased human activity on the natural environment are also greater than ever.

This role-playing activity focuses on just one environmental impact created by human activity: acid rain. Using information provided in Web sites established by the United States Environmental Protection Agency and state environmental agencies, conduct some field work that will help you prepare for one of the roles listed below. Be prepared to talk about the effects acid rain may have on your character, and to present arguments for, or against, policies to control acid rain.

U.S. Environmental Protection Agency program on acid rain (WWW 1.21).

Massachusetts Department of Environmental Protection
(an example of a state environmental agency)   (WWW 1.22).

Choose one of the following roles for the class discussion:
1. farmer
2. coal miner
3. factory owner
4. recreational fisherman
5. forester
6. architect
7. municipal health agent
8. resident of southeastern Canada
9. resident of a steel producing city

The instructor may wish to group individuals to jointly prepare a mock public hearing. Those individuals who play roles where their livelihoods could be negatively impacted by strict environmental regulations regarding acid rain may comprise one group. Another group could be those whose livelihoods could be positively impacted with more stringent regulations. A third group might approach the debate from a personal health perspective. Another group of may represent the regulating authority that would rule whether or not the environmental regulations should be strengthened.

ADDITIONAL WEB SITES FOR STUDYING ABOUT GEOGRAPHY, CULTURE, AND THE ENVIRONMENT:
The Web site for the *Association of American Geographers* contains information on the nature of geography, educational resources, and careers in geography. (WWW 1.23).

For a complete listing of the *National Geographic* sponsored Geographic Alliance Network sites. (WWW 1.24).

Worldwatch Institute is one of the leading non-profit public environmental policy research organizations in the United States. (WWW 1.25).

ADDITIONAL READINGS:
deSouza, Anthony R., et. al., *Geography for Life*, (Washington, D.C.: National Geographic Research & Exploration, 1994),

Huntington, Samuel, *The Clash of Civilization and the Remaking of the World Order*, (New York: Simon & Schuster, 1996).

McLuhan, Marshall, and Powers, Bruce, *The Global Village: Transformation in World Life and Media in the 21st Century*, (New York: Oxford University Press, 1993).

Postel, Sandra, *Air Pollution, Acid Rain, and the Future of Forests*, (Washington, D.C.: Worldwatch Institute, 1984), Worldwatch Paper #58.

PART FIVE: LAND AND LAND USE IN THE RURAL SECTOR
FOOD AND SHELTER:
GETTING DOWN THE BASICS OF LIFE

GOALS: To experience different cultural and economic conditions in rural regions with an emphasis on the diffusion of domesticated animals, traditional rural housing, and how commercial agriculture meets the global food needs.

ACTIVITIES: There are three activities for Part Five. First, you will travel the continents and study the domestication of animals. The focus of the second activity is a field study of folk architecture in the Great Plains. The third section allows you to take a look at the human and environmental impacts of aquaculture as a growing segment of world agribusiness.

ACTIVITY 5.1: How Now, Black and White Cow?   Livelihoods of Rural People.

INTRODUCTION: Have you ever wondered why it is that most of the dairy cattle you see are black and white spotted Holsteins? For many of us living in industrialized societies, the closest we get to livestock is taking a Sunday drive along a country road on the fringes of suburbia. If you have (and you can admit this) mooed at a cow standing along a fence line chewing its cud, chances are you were not raised on a farm.   In fact, less than three percent of the U.S. labor force lives on farms.

Urbanites are dependent on rural dwellers for food supplies and for most of us, the closest we get to harvesting our food is picking a can of peas from the grocers shelves or selecting an anonymous cut of meat from the butcher counter.   Unless you were born in an agricultural region, you are probably unfamiliar with livestock and how they developed and diffused from their source regions. To learn more about the diffusion of livestock from Ankole-Watusui (cattle) to Zhongwei (goats), visit Oklahoma State University's ***Breeds of Livestock*** Web site (WWW 5.1) This informative site will allow you to travel all over the world and discover how environmental conditions as well as the influences of local resources, diffusion, and historical inertia have contributed to the contemporary character of domesticated animals that provide food and fiber to billions of people.

Once at the ***Breeds of Livestock*** site, connect to the Regions page. Scroll down to the bottom of the page and click on Breed Home Page and read through this short introductory section. Then step back to the main page and click on the map in the area you are want to study. Your choices include: Africa, Asia, the British Isles, Continental Europe, North America, South America, and Oceania. You may select any or all of these regions and read about the types of livestock found in these areas, their origins and diffusion, as well as view images of each breed. While you may go into greater detail in your discussion of global livestock, we have selected some examples to consider for each region.   Each breed selected here has distinct geographic qualities and provides greater insight into the dynamics of animal domestication and diffusion. Certainly all of the breeds mentioned in this web site are interesting and, as time allows, you may wish to do some further exploration of the site on your own. When you have completed your research in each region, you should consider the following general questions.

Activity 5.1 Field Work

1. How have natural environments influenced the domestication and development of animal breeds?

2. How has diffusion changed the distribution of animals within regions and across throughout the world?

3. How have cultural preferences and changing economies affected breed popularity and distributions?

AFRICA
Cattle

Ankole (known as Ankole-Watusi in North America) *Can Cows Really do the Bossy Nova?*

1. How did the Ankole-Watusi earn its name---can they really dance? How are they related to the Ankole cattle of Africa and how are they similar or different?

2. Why have Ankole-Watusi cattle been raised mainly for their milk rather than their meat? How are milking practices between the two breeds different and why?

3. What role did zoos and game parks play in the diffusion of the Ankole-Watusi? What roles have the natural environment and cultural traditions played in the diffusion and development of the Ankole in Africa?

4. The photo of the Ankole-Watusi shown on this page gives you a good example of the large horns characteristic of this breed. How and why did this physical trait evolve? Why are the Ankole horns important to African cattle raisers?

N'dama *Fly By Night Cattle?*

1. How are these cattle different from the Ankole-Watusi in their physical characteristics as well as their geographic distribution?

2. Why is it important for African cattle raisers to improve their herds with trypanatotolerant breeds?

Goats

Boer Goat *A 300 Pound Goat --- We're Not Kidding!*

1. How did the Boer goat earn its name and what is its primary use?

2. Why do goats and cattle make a good combination when raised together in South Africa? Why didn't this livestock combination emerge in North America?

Sheep

Damara *Where Are Ewe?*

1. How did the environmental conditions of Namibia influence the development and utility of this breed?

ASIA
Cattle
Hallikar, Hariana, Kankrej, Sahiwal *We Have Four Kinds of Cattle on Draft*
Consider each of these south Asian cattle breeds, and answer the following questions.

1. If you were in need of a speedy long distance draft animal, which of these breeds would you select?

2. Why would draft cattle be so popular in this part of the world?

3. What makes the Sahiwal breed more versatile than the other three? Why has this breed experienced wider diffusionary patterns than the Hallikar, Hariana, or Kankrej?

Kholmogory *Hurry Up---These Cattle Are Russian!*
1. The photo example of the Kholmogory stands in stark contrast to the previous four breeds found in south Asia. What are the major environmental and use differences between the Kholmogory and the previously mentioned Asian cattle breeds?

Sanhe *So That's Where Ice Milk Comes From!*
1. What might the Sanhe and the Kholmogory share in terms of their adaptiveness to harsh environments?

2. How have the climatic effects of continentality in Inner Mongolia resulted in the hardy nature of Sanhe cattle?

Goats
Zhongwei *Getting Fleeced in China*
1. Goats are often associated with two things---poverty and poor agricultural areas. Why might the Zhongwei goat be well-suited to the physical geography of the Chinese steppe?

Other Asian Animals
Bactrian Camel, Dromedary Camel, Yak *Would You Walk a Mile for a Camel or a Yak?*
1. What are the major differences in environments between the animals commonly referred to as ships of the desert and those thought of as ships of the plateau?

2. Which type of camel are found in China? How are these camels different from those developed in Turkmenistan?

3. Why do you think there is no mention of Dromedary camels being use for meat?

4. Why would it not be a good idea to attempt to raise Dromedaries in the cold, moist climates in which Yaks might thrive?

5. How have each breed type contributed to their respective regions' demands for meat, milk, fiber, and transportation?

BRITISH ISLES
Cattle
Belted Galloway, Guernsey *Bring on the Cookies and Milk!*
With the Belted Galloway resembling a popular chocolate sandwich cookie and the Guernsey famous for their milk production, these two breeds seem like a natural combination! But, in fact, these two breeds are quite different.

1. Why have Geurnsey cattle been popular as milk producers and how did religion and soil bring this breed into existence?

2. What advantages do Galloway cattle have over other breeds and how have they adapted to their environment?

Goats
Bagot *Why It Is In Your Best Interest to Treat This Goat With Kid Gloves*
While Britain may not be as well known for its goats as it is for its sheep, the Bagot have an interesting and long history associated with the region.

1. How did the Bagot most likely develop in the British Isles and how did the breed influence local belief systems?

Sheep
Cotswold *Pulling the Wool Over Their Isles*
1. With over four dozen sheep breeds originating in the British Isles, you have many types to choose from. Many of these animals have names that double as toponyms and Cotswold sheep are just one example. How did this breed end up with this name?

Swine
Hampshire, Yorkshire *Hog Wild: Pigging Out in Britain*
The stories of both of these swine breeds echo that of native development and global diffusion. Both named for regions in England, they have had a profound influence on food production in many parts world, especially the United States.

1. How did the Industrial Revolution and hog production go ham in hand? Can you see any linkages between the development of factories and English agriculture such as the raisers of sheep and swine livestock?

2. How did the export of Hampshires to the United States affect the swine industry of the American Midwest?

CONTINENTAL EUROPE
Cattle
Herens, Holstein, Simmental *Cattle Call*
1. Many cattle breeds were developed in continental Europe with diverse purposes and histories including Herens, Holsteins, and Simmentals. Which of these might be best named demolition derby cattle and why are their numbers declining? Do you think this indicates a decline in transhumance as a grazing practice in Europe?

2. Today in the United States, Holsteins are the most numerous breed of dairy cattle. Where were Holsteins developed and how did they become so popular in the U.S.?

3. Let's say you decide to keep a Holstein cow for milking purposes. Based on the average per cow production in the United States, how many eight-ounce glasses of milk would your single black and white spotted cow produce during it's natural productive life (hint: a pound of milk is equal to a pint which is 16 ounces)? How does this help explain the chronic problem of over-supply of fluid milk on American markets given there are over nine million dairy cows in the United States?

4. Create a timeline of Simmental diffusion by starting with the first exports from Switzerland. Why has this breed spread throughout the world with greater success than any others?

Sheep
<u>Bovska</u>   *The Ups and Downs of Alpine Sheep Raising*
   1.   Why have the numbers of Bovska sheep declined since the 1950s?

   2.   What do geography and ears have in common when referring to the Bovska breed?

Swine
<u>Swallow-Bellied Mangalitza</u>   *Living Low On The Hog*
   1.   The popularity of domesticated animals is often determined by changing consumer tastes and preferences.   How has the popularity of the Swallow-Bellied Mangalitza been affected by contemporary diets?

NORTH AMERICA
Cattle
<u>Corriente,</u> <u>Senepol</u>   *Rope 'Em If You Got 'Em*
   1.   Corriente and Senepol cattle are good examples of how colonialism and animal diffusion are interrelated.   Where did each breed originate and where in North America did they develop?

   2.   What are some of the unique marketing conditions on St. Croix and why, even though cattle were present, did the island fail to develop any stockyards?

   3.   Where would you find descendents of the original Corriente cattle today and why?

Goats
<u>Myotonic,</u> <u>San Clemente</u>   *Goats for the Faint of Heart*
   1.   If you raise meat goats in Tennessee, why might they volunteer to faint?

   2.   It was recently announced that the United States Navy is phasing out their dairy farm operations near Annapolis, Maryland.   But how did the Navy get their goats---or better put, how did they get rid of them?

Sheep
<u>Hog Island, Tunis</u>   *Mutton Honey!*
   1.   Both Hog Island and Tunis sheep have their origins in colonial times but their fates have been quite different.   Which of these two American breeds is more rare and why? Do you see any irony in the role played by the Nature Conservancy on Hog Island and the decline of this breed?

   2.   Is sheep raising an important livestock industry in your region of the country? When was the last time you ate lamb or mutton---or have you ever?

SOUTH AMERICA
Cattle
<u>Nelore</u>   *Brazil is Nuts for Nelores*
   1.   What environmental similarities between Brazil and India have contributed to the success of the Nelore in South America?

Llama
<u>Llama</u>   *The Fiber of Their Being: The Multi-Purpose Llama*
   1. Llamas today are popular as pets although their heritage is much less glamorous. Why would the llama have been a useful animal to have on hand over that past 5,000 years?

OCEANIA
Cattle
Murray Grey *Getting Bullish on Australia*
   1. How did one man's prejudice against grey calves end up as the force behind the development of the Murray Grey?

   2. Where is one of the most favorable export markets for Murray Greys?

Sheep
Priangan *A Professional Athlete in Indonesia: Ram Merino?*
   1. What do Priangan sheep have in common with the Herens cattle of Switzerland? Do you have any ideas on why neither of these breeds have been popular outside their regions of origin?

Romney *Spinning a Sheep Tail*
   1. What are the qualities developed in the Romney breed that facilitated its success in New Zealand and the Falkland Islands and later to the United States?

Swine
Kuenkune *Pets or Meat?*
   1. Compare the Kuenkune to North America's Potbellied Pig. How did each of these breeds evolve from primarily rural meat animals to popular suburban pets?

Activity 5.2: There's No Place Like Home on the Range; Rural Settlement Forms

INTRODUCTION: Most often, folk (vernacular) architecture reflects localized geographic conditions in the types of building materials used, house style, as well as the arrangement of buildings and structures. Traditional homes may be made of adobe, thatch, hewn logs, or even animal hair. History, ethnicity, and the physical environment play a large role in the form and function of folk architecture.

Have you ever wondered why anyone would build a house out of sod? Could it be that there are no other alternatives? If you are accustomed to living in an urban setting, chances are your residence is constructed of modern building materials such as brick, concrete, block, metal, dimension lumber, or any combination of these.   Your home may even have been made in a factory and delivered to you. These conveniences of industrialized societies are not common in most parts of the world. Most of the world's population live in structures that were made by hand (often their own) and out of materials that are locally available to them such as mud, wattle, sod, handmade bricks, or even cloth.

Since most individuals have never lived in a sod house, we will use this type of construction as an example of folk architecture.   Sod houses played an important role in the settlement of the northern Great Plains region. To view some images of sod houses, go to the *Pioneer Camera* home page (WWW 5.2) and begin reading each description of the houses listed by clicking on Enter the Exhibit and selecting Sod Houses. Be sure to click on the "full page" option to see a larger and clearer image of each house, and to follow any links that are included in each narrative. For a complete picture of rural life in the Dakotas in the late 19th and early 20th centuries, be sure to take a few minutes and go to the <u>Farming Life</u> and <u>Prairie Society</u> links on the Exhibits page.

1. List the year in which each of the five houses was photographed. Which was the most recent and how was it different from the other examples of sod houses?

2. How would you describe the ethnicity of the sod house dwellers? Why do you think these people came to settle in the Dakotas? Would you expect to find sod houses in their respective homelands? Why or why not?

3. How did sod house dwellers on the plains demonstrate social stratification? In other words, what sorts of examples of social status and home improvements were they making to their sod houses to keep up with the Olsons?

4. Other than the Great Plains of North America, where else might you expect to find regions with sod houses as part of the cultural landscape?

Activity 5.3: Commercial Agriculture; There's Something Fishy Going On Here

INTRODUCTION: This chapter focuses on the dynamics of commercial agriculture. The activities listed below focus on aquaculture as an expanding sector in global agribusiness.

One of the most promising ventures for producing high protein food sources for the world is aquaculture. Since protein is one of the most important dietary components and is often missing or in low supply in the grain-based diets that are most common throughout the world, commercial fish production may help fill this critical need. Agribusiness expansion in aquaculture has been accelerating since the 1980s and should continue to do so as global demand continues to increase and fish harvests from natural water sources such as oceans and rivers continues to decline.

Aquaculture in the United States
Louisiana leads the United States in aquaculture with over 3,000 producers of fish for commercial purposes. Many other states have significant fish-farming agribusiness. For statistics on aquaculture for your state or the entire country from the United States Department of Agriculture, go Portland State University's *Government Information Project, Census of Agriculture* Web site (WWW 5.3). You may click on any state or "United States", which is highlighted in a box on the map. This information is also available at the county level if you choose an individual state. When the census data for the location you have chosen appear, select <u>Table 23 Fish Sales</u> and answer the following questions.

Activity 5.3 Field Work Questions

Part A
1. List the types of fish that are produced in your state and county. If your state has no aquaculture activities, go to Question 3.

223

2. What is the total dollar value of aquaculture in your state? How important do you think fish farming is to your state's economy?

3. If there is no aquaculture in your state, why do think this is the case?

4. If you want to see how your state or region fits within the broader aquaculture picture in the United States, go to the *United States Department of Agriculture Extension Service* Web site (WWW 5.4). This page will give you a brief overview of everything from crayfish crops in the Louisiana bayous to how to raise bass in Indiana on soybeans.

5. One of the largest fish crops in the United States in farm-raised catfish. More than five million pounds of the popular fish are produced each year. The *Catfish Institute* Web site (WWW 5.5), is baited with all sorts of information on catfish production and consumption. Visit the Catfish Institute to see how cat fish consumption varies by geography. Is your home state listed as one of the top consumers of catfish?

6. For a step by step illustrated tour of catfish farming, visit the Fish Pond at the Catfish Institute. In which four states are 95% of all farm-raised catfish produced? Are those the same top four states for consumption? Why do you think the patterns of production and consumption are different?

Part B
Global Aquaculture
Aquaculture is becoming an increasingly attractive agribusiness sector throughout the world as the demand for fish grows with populations and changing diets. To experience how the fish-farming industry is meeting market needs, go to the *Aquaculture Magazine* Web site (WWW 5.6) and click on the link for the World Aquaculture.

Select any of the articles listed below and answer the corresponding questions or discuss them as a group.

Australian Aquaculture Influenced by Asian Contracts
1. How has immigration changed the food culture of Australia and what has been the role of aquaculture in this dietary shift?

2. Which types of fish are being raised in Australia and what are some of the environmental problems that have been encountered?

Mexico's Shellfish Aquaculture
1. How has the physical environment both fostered as well as hindered the development of Mexican aquaculture?

2. What roles have politics (such as NAFTA) and education played in the expansion of fish-farming activities in Mexico?

Shrimp Farming Development in India. An Overview of Environmental, Socio-Economic, Legal and Other Implications
1. Where are shrimp produced in India and where are their export markets?

2. How has remote sensing been used to track aquaculture land use?

3. While the demand for shrimp is high in India, so are the environmental costs. Many examples are given in this article, list and discuss what you consider to be the three most significant problem areas.

Salmon Still A Major Part of Chile's Aquaculture Success
1. Where is Chile's aquaculture region? Why has this part of the country been so favorable for salmon production? (For additional background on the Chilean salmon industry, visit Web site WWW 5.7).

2. How have environmental conditions as well as infrastructure presented problems for aquaculture in Chile?

3. Why does Chile mainly focus on export markets for its fish products?

For an overview of world aquaculture, go to the *Food and Agriculture Organization* (FAO) site (WWW 5.8), select Fisheries and link to Review the State of World Aquaculture. After reviewing the article, you could write a short essay on the positive and negative impacts of aquaculture on the natural environment and the significance of aquaculture to rural areas and developing countries.

PART SIX
THE URBANIZING WORLD
ATTENTION ANY-MART SHOPPERS!

GOALS: What is "at issue" in the urbanizing world is the seemingly inevitable shift of commercial activities away from the central business district (CBD) and toward the suburbs. One of the largest segments of the economy that has steadily exited the downtown since the 1950s in favor of the suburbs is retailing. Through activities contained in this part, you will gain a better understanding of how your behavior as a consumer shapes the retail landscape and why "Main Street" retailers are disappearing from the shopping horizon.

ACTIVITIES: There are two major activities included for Part Six. The first section is devoted to exploring issues related to the decline of downtown shopping districts and strategies for their revival through Main Street programs. The second activity involves students conducting surveys of their personal shopping patterns and combining that data with the results for the rest of the class. After the group data is determined, students may choose to share their class results with students at other colleges and universities by posting their data to the *Virtual Field Guide* web site.

Activity 6.1: Main Street Gets Malled by the "Burbs"

INTRODUCTION: Shopping. Love it or hate it, we still have a need to shop. Some of us shop for reasons other than to obtain the necessities of life. For many, shopping is as much recreational as it is utilitarian. Prior to mass exodus of population and businesses from the CBD, when the majority of urbanites lived in a "walking city," virtually all shopping was oriented toward the downtown. Living and shopping on Main Street is getting more difficult to do these days. Through competition with the suburbs for shopping, employment, and entertainment dollars, many downtowns have become commercial relics. Those downtowns that continue to thrive have done so by capitalizing on their uniqueness as the historical heart of the region and by changing with times. Where you once had storefronts displaying shoes, furniture, or even groceries on Main Street, you now find gourmet coffee shops and upscale boutiques.

If you live in an area where you shop primarily in a downtown setting you are in a distinct minority. With the most common commuting pattern these days being from suburb to suburb, and the majority of the American population since 1990 living in suburbs, urban retailers are at a distinct disadvantage. The population shift to the suburbs has decreased foot traffic on downtown streets and directed consumer spending to malls, shopping centers and "big boxes" (e.g. large general merchandisers or large specialty stores with great depth of product lines). Downtowns do, however, have something to offer which suburban shopping centers and malls do not---historical context and organic character. When you visit a mall, think about how the form fails to follow function. For example, can you think of any shops inside your favorite mall with awnings or shutters on their storefronts? How about trees, fountains, or park benches---does your mall have any of these along its "main street?" What mall designers are attempting to do is replicate the outdoor downtown experience in an enclosed, climate controlled setting, often with plenty of free parking.

If we recreate the CDB in the form of a mall, why don't we just go back to shopping in the real downtowns and forsake the artifice of suburban shopping centers? Can traditional downtowns

227

once again become a mecca for shopping and entertainment as well as employment? One organization that is keenly involved with strategies to rejuvenate downtowns is the National Main Street Center, a branch of the National Trust for Historic Preservation. "Main Street" programs have been adopted by over 1,000 communities as ways to bring residents back to downtown. As you work through the problems in the following section, keep in mind the downtown situation you are most familiar with and compare its problems and progress with those in other locations.

Activity 6.1 Field Work
Part A

Using the *National Main Street Center (NMSC)* Web site (WWW 6.1) as your guide, work your way through this activity keeping in mind how the Main Street approach may or may not work in your community. Click on About Main Street and read the introductory section. Then follow the links for The Main Street Approach, The Decline of Main Street, The Importance of Downtown, and Main Street Communities. After reading through these sections, consider the following:

1. According to the NMSC, what element of the infrastructure has done the most economic damage to downtowns? Can you think of any local examples in your community where small towns have suffered due to changes in the transportation network?

2. Do you see the visual appearance of your downtown as a positive or negative force in its maintaining its economic significance?

3. Do you shop in a downtown setting? If so, what types of goods or services do you purchase downtown? Do you go downtown primarily to shop or for other purposes?

4. Do you know of any Main Street programs in your area? What, if any, differences do you see in the downtown since the program has been implemented?

5. Which of the three communities (Burlington, IA, Holland, MI, Port Gibson, MS) is most similar to your hometown? Do you think any of the approaches used by these cities would work well in your downtown area? Why or why not?

For many of you, when someone asks if you want to go shopping they perhaps are implying a trip to the local mall or shopping center and not the downtown. While Main Street programs have assisted in the revitalization of many downtown retail districts in the United States, most consumers still shop for such items as clothing, shoes, hardware, and household goods in suburban centers. Main Street programs are not panaceas for all downtowns. Some towns may be too small or too large for the Main Street approach or in some cases, the downtown revitalization effort lacks grassroots support and other crucial resources.

Have you ever thought about how your choices as a consumer and commuter help shape the landscape? Do you have any idea how many miles you drive everyday or how many shopping trips you make in a given day or week? Have you ever made a concerted effort to go out of your way to shop at locally owned stores rather than large chain retailers? Are there many "hometown" stores that survive in your town in the shadow of the Wal-Marts and Home Depots of the world? Begin thinking about a mental map of your shopping travels and later we will create a real map detailing your shopping habits and those of your fellow students.

Part B

For this section of Activity 6.1, explore your local retail landscape and create a shopping profile for you and your class. There are three things you will need to do. First, record you answers to the following questions about shopping in your community. Second, you will create a map of the local retail landscape. Third, combine your results with other class member and post these results to the ***Virtual Field Guide*** Web site so you can compare your experiences with students in other locations.

To begin, we need to identify the types of shopping opportunities you have in your region by linking to the ***International Council of Shopping Centers' (ICSC)*** Web site (WWW 6.2). Click on the "Research" link, select <u>Library</u> and then at the bottom of the page choose <u>Shopping Center Definitions</u>. Scroll down toward the end of the page until you reach the "Shopping Center Table." For each of the retail centers listed in Table 6.1 below, name any local examples as well as their locations that fit the descriptions. After you have listed the locations, note how many times you have visited these types of shopping centers in the past week.

Table 6.1

RETAIL CENTER	LOCAL EXAMPLES	LOCATIONS	TIMES VISITED THIS WEEK
Neighborhood Center			
Community Center			
Regional Center			
Superregional Center			
Fashion/Specialty Center			
Power Center			
Theme/Festival Center			
Outlet Center			
Downtown Stores			

Now that you have an inventory of local shopping centers, add to this list the downtown stores you have visited over the previous week.

Consider these questions:

1. Based on frequency of visits, which was the most popular shopping center (by name and type) for you and your classmates?

2. How did downtown shopping figure into the retail profile for this class? What were the most frequented stores by you and your classmates?

3. Do you feel the shopping opportunities in your town are satisfactory? What do you like best about shopping in your region? What types of changes if any would you like to see?

4. What is your favorite store to visit? Which is your least preferred and why?

5. On average, how many miles would you estimate you travel in a typical shopping trip?

6. Where do you normally shop for the following items (give store name and type of shopping center):

ITEM	STORE NAME	TYPE OF SHOPPING CENTER
Clothing		
Shoes		
Groceries		
Books (non-textbooks)		
Health and Beauty		
Home Electronics		
Music and Video		

The next step is to construct a map of these shopping center locations. Create a map of the area where you do the majority of your shopping. This will most likely be where you are currently living and where you regularly shop. Locate each of the shopping center types on the map. Then, draw circles around each, representing the primary trade area as defined in the tables on the *ICSC* Web page (WWW 6.2). You can use a simple compass to draw the circles but be sure to check the map scale to accurately delimit each trade area. You will need a map of your study area that can accommodate distances of at least 15 miles. If you do not have a ready-made map handy, you can create a map from various sites on the Internet including: the *Map Blast!* Web site (WWW 6.3) and the *Maps On Us* Web site (WWW 6.4).

Part C

When you have your map completed, answer the following questions:

1. Do any shopping center market areas overlap?

2. Is there any identifiable locational pattern of retailing that you can identify based on the map you have created (i.e., are the shopping opportunities located in certain areas or are they associated with specific transportation routes?)?

3. Why is it difficult for smaller shopping centers to compete against malls?

4. Do any of the shopping center market areas overlap a downtown retail district?

MAKING THE MOST OF YOUR CLASS RESEARCH

Now that you have created a shopping behavior profile for your class, you can compare your group to other college students by visiting the Virtual Field Guide web site. Go to the page for Part Six and click on the Travel Survey option. You will need to collect, summarize, and send the following information for your class by each of these categories:

University or College		
Percent Male		*These two should add to 100%*
Percent Female		
Average Age of Individuals in Class		
Percent On-Campus		*These two should add to 100%*
Percent Commuter		
Percent Who Use Transportation to Go Shopping		
- personal vehicle		
- public transportation		
- bicycle		
- other		
Most Frequently Visited Shopping Center Type		
Is There an Active Main Street Program in Your Town? (yes/no)		
Average Number of Miles Travelled per Typical Shopping Trip		
Most Popular Stores for:	Store	Type of Location
- clothing		
- shoes		
- books		
- health and beauty		
- home electronic		
- groceries		
- music and video		

You can e-mail your class results and they will be added to data from other college geography classes. After sending your information, compare the results to other classes if it is available. Is your group unique or fairly typical? Do you see any regional travel or shopping patterns across the United States? Do shopping habits vary depending on city size? How might urban geographers be able to use this type of information in transportation and land use planning? Are there any strategies downtown retailers could use to draw customers back from suburban shopping centers?

ADDITIONAL WEB SITES FOR STUDYING URBAN GEOGRAPHY

Urban Land Institute (WWW 6.5)
U.S. Malls Home page (WWW 6.6))
Mall of America (WWW 6.7)
King of Prussia Plaza (WWW 6.8)

231

PART SEVEN
THE GEOGRAPHY OF MODERN ECONOMIC CHANGE

GOALS: To classify countries according to their level of economic development and to see the correlation between development and the demographic transition. Second, to become aware of how industries adapt to change in order to survive in today's global economy. To recognize the range of basic business protocol in a selection of world cultures.

ACTIVITIES: Access and use data to classify countries by level of development, visit Ocean Spray Cranberries, Inc. in order to construct a corporate case study of adaptation and innovation, and study and test business protocols.

ACTIVITY 7.1: Are We There Yet? Classifications of Economic Development

INTRODUCTION: Countries of the world can be classified according to level of economic development, based on a broad array of socio-economic variables. Until fairly recently, many sources simply classified nations into *"developed"* and *"underdeveloped."* Sometimes they are referred to as the *"haves"* and *"have nots."* There are some problems using such a simple, two-category classification. First, there is the underlying implication of superiority and inferiority of the developed nations and underdeveloped nations, respectively. Secondly, many countries do not clearly fit into either of these two broad categories. For the purposes of this activity, the following four-fold classification will be used:

1. underdeveloped
2. developing
3. almost developed
4. developed

These economic stages correlate with the four stages of the demographic transition as outlined in Part 2, Chapter 5, of the de Blij and Murphy text.

Activity 7.1 Field Work

Choose a world country, and refer to **Central Intelligence Agency** Web site (WWW 7.1). Look up the requested data for your country, as per the categories of information in Table 7.1 below, and circle the numbers that apply to your country. Total the number of circles in each column.

    1. Where does your country best fit in terms of level of development?

Notes: Some countries may fall on the "boundary" between two of these stages of development. Also, the addition or subtraction of one or more variables could change a country's position within this classification. If different data sources are used, you may find different values for a particular variable. You should also be aware that the data changes over time. Try to stick with a single source of information, if possible. You should note any significant differences between data sources. A follow-up exercise would be for your class as a whole to make a choropleth world map of development based on your findings.

233

Table 7.1. COUNTRY DEVELOPMENT CLASSIFICATION

Country: _____ Data Source Used: _____

Variable	Underdeveloped	Developing	Almost Developed	Developed
Population Growth Rate (%)	> 3	2.1 - 3	1 - 2	< 1
Birth Rate (per 1000)	> 45	31 - 45	20 - 30	< 20
Population under Age 15	> 40%	31 - 40%	20 - 30%	< 20%
Infant Mortality Rate (per 1000 births)	> 100	51 - 100	10 - 50	< 10
Life Expectancy	< 55	55 - 64	65 - 70	> 70
Literacy Rate	< 70%	70 - 79%	80 - 90%	> 90%
G.D.P. (dollars per capita)	< 200	200 - 1,900	2,000 - 15,000	> 15,000
G.D.P. % Agriculture	> 40%	21 - 40%	10 - 20%	< 10%
% of Labor in Agriculture	> 30%	21 - 30%	10 - 20%	< 10%
Persons per Television*	> 500	101 - 500	10 - 100	< 10
TOTAL CIRCLES				
Conclusion (Check one)				

* Calculate Persons per Television Set by dividing the Total Country Population by the number of televisions.

ACTIVITY 7.2: "Berry" Good Business! Adapting to Change in the Business World

INTRODUCTION: In order to survive in today's competitive business world, corporations must constantly adapt to ever changing demographics, markets, preferences, trends, and technological innovations. One of the better examples of market adaptation is the story of Ocean Spray Cranberries, Inc. This is a Fortune 400 company that made a $1.4 billion business out of a tiny, bitter berry. Compile a case study of the company by visiting *Ocean Spray Cranberries, Inc.* (WWW 7.2).

Part A

Click on their *"Timeline of Innovation."* List what key innovations occurred in the following years:

1930: _____

1939: _____

1942: _____

1951: _____

1952: _____

1963: _____

1977: _____

1981: _____

1993: _____

1995: _____

Part B

Click *"Company Profile."* Go to the last section that lists where Ocean Spray's facilities are located. On figure 7.1.a, label the U.S. states that have cranberry receiving stations. On Figure 7.1.b, label the states with processing and bottling plants. Why do you think these areas stand out on both maps?

Figure 7.1.a States with Cranberry Receiving Stations

Figure 7.1.b States with Cranberry Processing and Bottling Plants

Part C

Read more about the cranberry by clicking on the page "*Cranberries and Citrus*," and then go to the page "<u>Cranberry Fun Facts</u>" to complete the Cranberry Quiz.

1. True/False: Cranberries are a native American fruit.

2. Why did sailors in colonial days keep cranberries on board their ships?

3. Cranberries grow well in what type of soil?

4. True/False: Cranberries grow in water.

5. How many states are major cranberry producers?

6. Which country in South America grows cranberries?

7. What is the average number of cranberries per pound?

8. What percentage of cranberries are consumed during Thanksgiving week?

9. What percentage of the world's cranberries are sold by Ocean Spray?

10. True/False: Cranberries are quite suitable for wine making.

In summary, the cranberry industry is a good example of adaptation and innovation. Can you cite other industries that have had to adapt to change? In what ways have they adapted?

ACTIVITY 7.3: Sayonara To Faux Pas!

INTRODUCTION: In today's world, many businesses compete in the global market. This greater exposure to foreign cultures has led to some embarrassing business *faux pas* (blunders).

This activity demonstrates a few of the cultural *"land mines"* that one could accidentally step on when conducting business abroad. Remember, no one culture is *"right,"* or *"better"* than another. But customs and expectations of foreign hosts are often different from our own. Those who have taken the time to learn about the cultural differences stand a much greater chance of business success.

Activity 7.3 Field Work

Take **Interface JAPAN's** simple yes/no five-question *"Intercultural Training and Business Protocol Quiz"* :

1. Is it appropriate to arrive 10 minutes early to a business appointment in Japan?

    _____ YES   _____ NO

2. In a meeting with Japanese business people, you make a joke in English and laugh. Is this behavior appropriate?

    _____ YES   _____ NO

3. When your Japanese friend asks you to go to a bar after work, you say, "I can't because I want leave soon." Is that a reasonable response?

    _____ YES   _____ NO

4. Visiting a Japanese company,you exchange business cards with your Japanese colleague and then sit down. Have you followed the correct business etiquette?

    _____ YES   _____ NO

5. At a presentation with Japanese people you ask, "Do you understand?" Is that a polite question?

    _____ YES   _____ NO

To check your answers, go to the **InterfaceJAPAN** Web site (WWW 7.3).

How many out of the five did you have as correct? _____

If you answered all five correctly, *Subarashi!* (Great!) This quiz focused strictly on Japanese business protocol. Here are some other brief guides to follow when you are conducting business in other parts of the world according to the celebrated international business expert Roger Axtell in his best-selling book: <u>Do's and Taboos Around the World</u>.

Europe: What would be mildly bad manners at home (gum chewing, talking with hands in pockets, back slapping, etc.) are cardinal sins on the Continent. Europeans tend to be more formal than most Americans. Punctuality is a must, especially in Northern Europe.

Africa: This continent is divided into three sub-regions: northern nations bound together by language (Arabic), religion (Islam), and resources (oil); middle Africa (black multicultures); and South Africa (long time Dutch/English orientation). North Africa generally follows Arabic protocol, gestures, etiquette (don't use your left hand!), and behavior. The nations in middle Africa are oriented to a myriad of black multicultures, and it is impossible to generalize about such a complex region. Because of the recent downfall of the apartheid system, the once strong European (Dutch/English) cultural connections are in a state of flux.

Asia & the Pacific World: No region of the world has a greater variety and diversity of languages, races, and religions, than Asia. Most Asians are extremely polite. The worst mistake one could make in business is to allow your foreign host to "lose face." Business cards are swapped at a pace that put children trading baseball cards to shame! Cards should be printed in both English and the local language. You should be punctual for appointments, but don't be offended if your hosts are late. When doing business in Japan, it is often essential to have a strong contact with an established Japanese firm. Due to the cultural origins, directness, and informality of its citizens, Australia is probably the one nation in this region where Americans feel the most "at home" when conducting business.

Central & South America: Although we tend to over-generalize about Latin America, do recognize that there are many differences in customs and behavior. One behavioral aspect that takes some getting used to by U.S. citizens is that Latin Americans tend to stand close during conversations. Latin Americans are warm and friendly people. Punctuality is not closely adhered to in this region.

The Caribbean: This is another region with considerable diversity in languages, races, and cultures. Casual dress and less formal behavior are commonplace.

Canada: Canada is comprised of many different ethnic groups, and while customs are generally similar, there are some differences. This is particularly true in Quebec, where language is a very sensitive issue. Most Canadians tend to be somewhat more conservative than most U.S. citizens.

Having read these protocol summaries, have you noticed any of these behaviors depicted on television or in the movies? Have you had any personal experiences where you personally made a mistake in protocol? Here's a tip when hosting an English guest: Don't serve corn with a meal. The English view corn as animal feed! To avoid these kinds of mistakes, see

> Brad Bowerman's *Geography World* site for a huge list of links to cultural sites (WWW 7.4).

> View the site *Gestures in Cultures*, to learn about body language around the world (WWW 7.5).

ADDITIONAL WEB SITES ON THE GEOGRAPHY OF MODERN ECONOMIC CHANGE:

For a listing of many sites on China's business and trade, see *China on the Net* (http://www.kn.pacbel.com/wired/China/hotlist) (WWW 7.6).

For a good example of how a community advertises itself to compete for industrial economic development, see the informative website for *Taunton, Massachusetts* (http://www.ci.taunton.ma.us/info.htm) (WWW 7.7).

Need detailed, up-to-date information on a particular country's economic structure and trends? View the *World Bank* website's "*Country Briefs*"

ADDITIONAL WEB SITES ON THE GEOGRAPHY OF MODERN ECONOMIC CHANGE:

For a listing of many sites on China's business and trade, see ***China on the Net*** (WWW 7.6).

For a good example of how a community advertises itself to compete for industrial economic development, see the Web site for the town of ***Taunton, Massachusetts*** (WWW 7.7).

Need detailed, up-to-date information on a particular country's economic structure and trends? View the "*Country Briefs*" page on the ***World Bank*** Web site. (WWW 7.8).

Pennsylvania's industrial trends are described in the Research Brief entitled "*Industry Trends in Pennsylvania*" on the ***Pennsylvania State Data Center*** Web site (WWW 7.9).

What is the impact of economic growth on a developing country? See "Exploring the Health Impact of Economic Growth, Poverty Reduction, and Public Health Expenditure," at the ***World Health Organization*** Web site (WWW 7.10).

ADDITIONAL READINGS:

Axtell, Roger E., *Do's and Taboos Around the World*, (New York: John Wiley & Sons, Inc., 1990), 2nd ed.

Axtell, Roger E., *The Do's and Taboos of International Trade*, (New York: John Wiley & Sons, Inc., 1991).

Jones, K., and Simmons, J., *The Retail Environment*, (New York: Routledge, 1990).

Renner, Michael, Swords Into Plowshares: Converting to a Peace Economy, (Washington, D.C.: Worldwatch, 1990)

PART EIGHT
THE POLITICAL IMPRINT
ALL NATIONS GREAT AND SMALL

GOALS: The purpose of these activities is to bring the relative abstraction of politics to the reality of everyday life. We will explore and discuss political boundaries, challenge the conventional notion of what makes a nation, and examine the tenuous existence of nations without states. All these topics should bring to you new perspectives on the dynamics of political geography and the role it plays in shaping your world.

ACTIVITIES: Our virtual tour of the political landscape includes three activities. First, we look at the lines that bind – the geography of boundaries. Next, prepare for a tour of some of the tiniest "nations" on earth as they exist in reality or only on mental maps. Finally, we look at stateless nations facing difficult political and geographic odds.

ACTIVITY 8.1: Political Culture and the Evolving State
Bounded and Determined: Taking Political Boundaries to the Edge

INTRODUCTION: Every single day, perhaps without any awareness on your part, you cross a variety of political boundaries. Would you know when you leave one local voting precinct and venture into another or traverse one Congressional District and enter another? The boundaries you are probably most familiar with are those of city limits, township, county, state and national boundaries. What you may not know is that most of those boundaries have changed over time and in the past, may have been a serious point of contention. If the only things certain in life are death and taxes, you might want to add boundaries to that list because humans are very territorial and that's where all the troubles start. The following questions all deal with identifying geographic boundaries at different scales. We will begin with boundary lines in your part of the world and expand our investigation to a global scale. Some of the questions require little more than using your knowledge of local conditions but when possible it is recommended that you back up your answers with maps or documentation. A local city, county, state, topographical or U.S. Census map may provide the verification you need.

Activity 8.1 Field Work Questions
Part A

1. Name your county of residence and all counties with which it shares borderlines. How would you best describe the character of the boundary? For example, does it appear that the boundaries are based on physical environment such as water courses or mountain ridges or are they geometric survey lines that do not follow any obvious natural features or perhaps a combination of both?

2. Do you know of any boundary disputes in your state, county or community? What part, if any, have the region's physical geography played in these disputes?

Part B

Boundary line disputes have played a major part in conflicts at many levels from family feuds to full-scale wars. The following list of web sites will provide you with some examples of how arguments over territory and boundaries have resulted in a variety of changes to the political landscape.

The Iowa and Missouri Dispute

The Iowa Honey War site (WWW 8.1) If you had never heard about a series in incidents in 1839 that nearly brought Iowa and Missouri to the brink of war you are not alone. With such battle cries as "Death to the Pukes" and armed with such lethal weapons as kitchen utensils, residents near the disputed boundary between the two states were prepared to do battle over honey. That's right— honey.

1. How did such a conflict develop and how was it resolved and why was the final agreement much sweeter for Iowa?

The U.S.-Canada Boundary in the Pacific Northwest: The Pig War

The National Park Service San Juan Island National Historical Park Web sites (WWW 8.2), (WWW 8.3), (WWW 8.4)

The United States and Canada share the longest unfortified border in the world. While on the surface it appears that the two countries are fairly comfortable with this peaceful relationship, in the past, the border has been a source of much contention. After the dispute over one section of the border involving British Columbia was resolved one piece of the United States ended up as an enclave within Canada.

2. Where would you find this unusual piece of real estate?

3. Can you think of any reason why the United States would fight in the "Pig War" to retain this relatively tiny chunk of territory?

4. What are the differences between "British" and "English" camps and what precipitated the name variations?

5. Do you think British and English should be used interchangeably—why or why not?

The Baarle-Nassau/Baarle-Hertog Dispute

Professor Barry Smith's *Baarle-Nassau/Baarle-Hertog* Web site (WWW 8.5) No, not the Nassau located in the Caribbean. These "islands" are on dry land in Belgium and the Netherlands.

6. What makes these enclaves so unique?

7. How were they formed and what attempts have been made over the past to resolve this conundrum?

Explore other border issues with the *International Boundary News Database* Web site (WWW 8.6) If there is a boundary issue somewhere in the world, it is probably cited in the International Boundary News Database. You can access the database by simply entering location names and submitting your search request. When database completes the search it will list all the boundary issues associated with the locations you have chosen. Read through the search results and list and discuss what you believe are the major border issues.

8. How would you classify the boundary you chose (see page 350 in your text for a discussion of "Origin-Based Classification)?

Activity 8.2: State Organization and National Power
Micro-Minis: Skirting the Issues of Statehood

INTRODUCTION: What does it take to create a country? Is it political or military power over a geographic territory? Do you need a minimum number of people to qualify? Or do you become a state because others recognize your legal right to exist? For some smaller states, retaining their identity, or for that matter creating one, can present some problems. Many states have populations of less than one million residents. These are ministates and despite their small size, they manage to function as fully legitimate political entities yet wield little influence in global affairs. Then there are the microstates. Microstates may or may not have any political or geographic raison d'etre, but exist nonetheless. Some microstates are self-proclaimed nations created by individuals, groups, or even corporations such as the "Republic of Ceurvo Gold," established by a tequila manufacturer. In fact, some microstates exist only in the minds of their creators or on the Internet such as the "Aeldarnian Empire." And then there is the "Kingdom of Talossa" which was created by a high school student and territorially consisted of his bedroom. Some say the world is getting smaller. Let's take a look and see.

Activity 8.2 Field Work

Prepare to take a magical mystery virtual field trip to an amazing variety of microstates.

> To begin your journey, go to the ***Micronations*** Web site (WWW 8.7) and read the section titled, "What are Micronations?" Next, scroll down to the list of micronations and answer the questions for the micronations listed below.

1. <u>Breckenridge</u>: Why did this town declare itself a "kingdom?"

2. <u>Christiania</u>: Exactly how would you describe this "social experiment?" Would such a community survive in the United States? Why?

3. <u>Conch Republic</u>: How did Border Patrol action bring this microstate out of its shell? (Be sure to the visit the ***Cyber Conch*** Web site too. WWW 8.8).

4. <u>Minerva, Republic of</u>: Why did this "republic" fail to keep its head above water?

5. <u>Morac-Songhrati-Meads, Republic of</u>: Where is the "Humanity Sea" and exactly how human is it?

6. <u>Mosquito Shore and Nation</u>: Who have been the main political players that have wrestled for this territory for the past 300 years?

7. <u>Navassa Island</u>: What does the self-proclaimed king have to rule over on Navassa and why might the Coast Guard want to take his throne? Tour the island via its ***Navassa Island*** Web site (WWW 8.9) and follow the link for <u>History</u> for more information.

8. <u>Seborga, Principality of</u>: Seborga has been a microstate for over 1000 years. Why is it still struggling for recognition? Travel to the principality via its ***Principato di Seborga*** Web page (WWW 8.10).

9. <u>Winneconne</u>: What does Winneconne have in common with Breckenridge?

243

Activity 8.3: Multinationalism on the Map
States of Minds and Hearts: UNPO Members

INTRODUCTION: The Unrepresented Nations and Peoples Organization (UNPO) provides a forum for groups who are not represented in traditional supranational bureaucratic institutions such as the United Nations (UN). For those nations without a state, the UNPO offers assistance and guidance for self-help programs and adheres to philosophy of progress through non-violent measures. Who are the more than 50 members of the UNPO and what are they doing to ease the plight of their peoples?

Activity 8.3 Field Work

The *UNPO* Web site (WWW 8.11) is the starting point for this activity. Go to the UNPO home page and click on <u>What is the UNPO?</u>.

1. Based on what you have read, how is the UNPO different from the UN?

Next, go back to the main page and select <u>Members of UNPO</u>. Select any one of the member nations *excluding* those peoples who reside in the United States and answer the following questions (helpful hint: if possible, you should print the member's page for future reference).

Note the UNPO member you have chosen to study: _____

2. Describe the geographic location.

3. What ethnic group(s) are included in this area?

4. What types of economic activities take place in this region?

5. How did this group of people survive to this point and what are the major challenges for their future as a nation with or without a state?

6. Why do you believe the UNPO you have selected has not been given independence or been recognized as a nation and what geographic factors are involved?

7. Were you surprised to learn that there are UNPO members in the United States?

Go through the list of UNPO members and pick out those nations that are currently living within the U.S. borders. List those members below and answer the following questions.

8. List the UNPO member nations that reside within the political boundaries of the United States.

9. Where are these nations located within the United States?

10. What, if any, do these peoples have in common?

11. In the best case scenario, what do you see as the future for each of these groups? Do you think they will ever become nations with a state or will they continue to be assimilated into the host culture? Why do you think this is the case?

12. Are there any parallels you see between the UNPO members in the United States and the other member nation you selected? If so, what are the similarities as well as the differences?

PART NINE
SOCIAL GEOGRAPHIES
OF THE MODERN WORLD --
GRRRL POWERLESS

GOALS: The focus of this section is on gender and the geography of inequality. There are three activities included for these subjects all of which are key points for Chapter 31 in Part Nine. Each of the activities is designed to challenge students to look deeper into cultural differences through the lens of gender.

ACTIVITIES: The first activity centers on gender and demographics, and examines the status of women in several countries. It asks students to compare their lifestyles to those in other locations. For example, Figure 31.1 in the de Blij and Murphy text illustrates the spatial differences between male and female life expectancies. Students will look for demographic clues in other statistics which help explain life expectancy patterns. The second activity follows up on the demographic study by examining female infanticide and other reproductive rights topics related to the status of women. The final part of this activity looks at women in the workplace with emphasis on women in the family economy and women laborers in the third world.

Activity 9.1: Gender and the Geography of Inequality; No Great Life Expectations

INTRODUCTION: A quick review of de Blij and Murphy's Figure 31-1, "World Female Life Expectancy over Males, shows that three countries, Bangladesh, India, and Pakistan, are the only countries in the world where females do not outlive males. Various factors have been attributed to life expectancy differences between males and females but generally the world pattern of longer lives for females have been explained by unhealthy lifestyle choices made by males. Why are females in these three countries not enjoying longer lives? Are some countries less favorable for female survival? What factors enable men to live longer than women? To explore these questions, let's proceed to the following activities that focus on the gender-based demographics of life expectancies.

ACTIVITY 9.1 Field Work
Follow the web links for each of these countries and be prepared to discuss your findings.

BANGLADESH: Poverty brings suffering to both males and females but in the case of Bangladesh, the effects on the lives of women are particularly harsh. For a brief introduction to some of the demographic variables that can be used to explain life expectancy differences by gender, go to the ***Novartis Foundation for Sustainable Development*** Web page on poverty in Bangladesh (WWW 9.1). After reading the short narratives and reviewing the data included in the two tables, answer the following questions.

1. What percent of the total Bangladeshi population live in rural areas? How does this contribute to lower life expectancies for women? Which of the factors found in the table titled, "Female-Male Gaps in Bangladesh" best supports your explanation and why?

2. How does the natural environment conspire with desperate social conditions to further lower the quality of life for both males and females in Bangladesh? Can you think of any solutions to help mitigate these hazards?

If there is one condition that is genderless it is hunger. No matter whether you are a woman or a man, when you are in need of food, the hunger pangs are equally debilitating. But due to the unique role of women in the family, they are in fact at greater risk to the effects of malnutrition. In Bangladesh, if a woman is not receiving adequate food, her children, born and unborn, as well as herself, are at higher risk. For more insight into the issue of hunger and gender, go to the "Women's Health and Nutritional Security in Bangladesh" page at the *Novartis Foundation* Web Site (WWW 9.2). After reading this article, answer the following questions concerning health, education, marriage, and the legal status of women in Bangladesh.

3. How have gender inequities in health care resulted in differing qualities of life for children? In Bangladesh, who eats "last and least"? Think about the role of gender and food in your home. Is this Bangladeshi culture trait similar to what you experience in your family? How?

4. According to the World Bank, what factors are responsible for the high maternal mortality rate suffered by Bangladeshi women? If you were hired as a consultant and were asked to target one of these variables that could be most easily remedied, which would you choose and why?

5. What is the maternal mortality rate in the United States? To find this statistic, refer to Table 3 on the UNICEF *Country Estimates of Maternal Mortality* Web site (WWW 9.3). What are some of the factors you believe account for the differences in maternal mortality rates between Bangladesh and the United States? List the countries with maternal mortality rates lower than those of the United States. Why do you think these countries are doing a better job of ensuring safer motherhood than the U.S.? Which countries have the highest maternal and lowest mortality rates and what factors do you think contribute to these conditions for women?

6. How does violence against women translate into a health and cultural issue in Bangladesh?

7. Was anyone in your family denied a public school education because of their gender? Why would this happen to young girls in Bangladesh? What are the long-term consequences of lack of adequate education for females in Bangladesh? How is denial of education justified in this culture? Have you ever heard these arguments against educating women in the United States and why?

8. How do religion, early onset of puberty, and the status of females combine to lower life expectancies and qualities of life for young Bangladeshi women?

9. Widowhood in any situation is very difficult, but why are Bangladeshi women at great risk if they lose their husbands?

10. If Bangladeshi women are "equal" under the law, how is it they are burdened with great inequities?

11. Follow the Purdah link in the final paragraph of the *Novartis* Web site. What is Purdah and how does it affect the lives of Bangladeshi women (WWW 9.4)?

After reading the previous materials and giving considerable thought to the living conditions experienced by Bangladeshi women, what do you see as their future? Do you foresee life female expectancies to increase, decrease, or stay the same in the future and why?

ACTIVITY 9.2: Mothers and Daughters of India

INTRODUCTION: Many cultural, economic, and political factors influence family size and composition. Reproductive rights are not automatically associated with individual freedoms in many parts of the world. In regions where females are considered less than equals, and male children are preferred, women and girls often find themselves in perilous situations. Such is the case in India, where men outnumber women, an unusual demographic in a world where females generally experience longer life expectancies and sex ratios at birth are virtually 50/50. Why do males outnumber females in India? Part of the explanation lies in family planning decisions that are shaped by the status of women.

While working through the activities below, keep in mind how powerful cultural belief systems such as religion and the traditional role of women play in the composition of families and gender preference.

ACTIVITY 9.2 Field Work

Part A

We begin our journey to India by visiting the *Women of the World* Web site (WWW 9.5). Begin reading and click on <u>Please begin with the introduction</u>. When you reach the bottom of the page, begin your review of social conditions by clicking on <u>India</u>, read the <u>Overview</u> section then go back to the web links box at the top or bottom of the page and click on each of the following: <u>Population and Family Planning, Contraception, Sterilization, Other Reproductive Health Matters.</u>

1. What types of incentives does the Indian government offer those who are willing to participate in family planning programs? Why would this appeal to many communities in India?

2. How does the government and private industry work together to distribute contraceptives? Why might a similar program in the United States meet with some resistance?

3. Who are more likely to be sterilized in India -- males or females, and why do you think this would be the prevailing trend? How does the government reward persons who choose to be sterilized? Does the United States government reward its citizens in comparable ways for family planning decisions? (Hint: Think income taxes!)

4. What are "dowry deaths" and how is this representative of the status of women in India?

Part B

Dowry deaths are but one hazard to growing up female in India. Some girls never have the chance to be born because the fetus is aborted based on ultrasound tests indicating the unborn child is female. Selectively aborting fetuses by gender is called "foeticide". Female infanticide, foeticide, and other factors contribute to a growing problem of missing girls in India. Simply put, there are millions of females "missing" from the Indian population, women who statistically should be a part of the demographic profile of the country. For a cartographic representation of the unbalanced sex-ratio problem in India, go to U.N.I.C.E.F.'s Web Site that addresses *Gender Equity in India* (WWW 9.6).

1. What can you surmise about "missing women" from the spatial pattern on the map?

2. Which Indian state has the highest number of "missing women"? Keep this location in mind as you read the next section.

Part C

Next, go to the ***Hinduism Today*** web site and read, "Will India's Ban on Prenatal Sex Determination Slow Abortion of Girls?" (WWW 9.7), and answer the following questions. (Note: This site contains an entire collection of articles, but the following questions focus on just this one article.)

1. How have advances in medical technologies resulted in the proliferation of female foeticide in India and why are some ultrasound clinics going "underground?"

2. What reasons do "pro-selective abortion" advocates present when supporting female foeticide? Do you agree with any of these arguments and why?

3. How has emphasis on the male child influenced the status of girls and women in India? Do you see any parallels between these issues in India and China and why?

4. What is *stri dana* and how does the dowry system place females in peril in India?

5. Which state in India has the greatest prevalence of dowry practices? With the UNICEF "missing women" in India map you previously viewed, what do these two issues have in common?

6. Hinduism is practiced by hundreds of millions of Indians. How do Hindus view abortion and why does the practice continue despite the religious contradictions?

7. Step back from India for just a moment. Think about the different values placed on gender where you live. Do you believe males are valued above females in your country? If so, list some examples, and if not, explain why.

Part D

At this point, you should have a good understanding of the risks involved in being an Indian woman but what would a female visitor to India encounter as she travels the countryside? Become a virtual woman tourist in India by going to the ***Hot Wired*** Web page (WWW 9.8) You'll receive advice as a female traveler. Be sure to take a side trip and click on <u>Indian Women</u> near the beginning of the article and answer the following.

1. What sorts of interactions with Indian men are women tourists warned about and how are they advised to deal with unwanted social situations—or why you shouldn't go barefoot on a bus?

2. What is "Eve teasing" in India and are these behaviors unique to this part of the world?

3. Given the description of women in Indian society (<u>Indian Woman</u>), why do you think female foreigners are treated so differently?

4. While this article mentions many difficulties for women travelers in India, what, if any, are considered to be the perks? Based on this information, whether you are male or female, would you be interested in visiting India---why or why not?

ACTIVITY 9.3: Caution: Women at Work

INTRODUCTION: The majority of the world's work force is composed of women. Women work in fields, factories, mines, oceans, forests, deserts, and in the home. Working conditions vary wildly and are more commonly unfavorable than not. In most countries, female laborers are paid less and work more hours than their male counterparts thus having direct economic consequences on the welfare of families. To explore the challenges faced by women in the world labor force, we will examine the lives of women in Pakistan, women as food producers, and a case study of a female factory worker in Mexico.

ACTIVITY 9.3 Field Work
Part A
We begin by visiting the *First to Rise Last to Sleep* Web site (WWW 9.9), which details the lives of women in Pakistan. Consider the following questions.

1. How has geography affected the status of women in Pakistan and how is this reflected in the labor force?

2. How are prospects for urban women in Pakistan different from those living in rural areas?

3. Who are the women of the Pakistani middle class and how are their lives different from other women in the country?

Part B
Many women, including those living in Pakistan, make major contributions to the family economy. Whether she is assembling clothes in an apparel factory or canning foods for the family's consumption, women provide direct support for themselves and her families. Women as food producers are often overlooked as a part of the overall economy. For a closer look at how much of the world's labor is generated by a nearly invisible class of workers – women in the developing world – go to the United Nations' *Food for the Future* Web page (WWW 9.10). Read "Women as Food Producers" and consider the following questions.

1. What do you think accounts for longer working days for women versus men? Compare your own experiences to those mentioned in the article. Do you think women in your community work more or less hours per day than men? How do you think these work schedules affect family life?

2. How does the lack of a male head of household impact the welfare of many families in terms of malnutrition? Were you surprised by this revelation why or why not?

3. Why are men migrating to urban areas and how does the absence of men complicate land tenure issues?

4. How are reproductive rights and adequate access to food interrelated?

5. Why does the United Nations argue that the world is headed for an "absolute food shortage" and what solutions do they offer?

6. Why is it difficult for many rural women in Africa to qualify for credit and how would this affect food production?

Part C

Many women spend most of their days not in fields but on assembly lines. The diffusion of manufacturing from industrialized regions to developing areas in an effort to capture cheap labor, has resulted in a new class of working poor. In Mexico, "maquiladoras," low-wage, low-skill factories that locate along the U.S.-Mexico border, provide employment for thousands of women. The story of one such woman, Maria Ilbarra, is told in "The Life of a Maquiladora Worker" on the *Pacific News Service* Web site (WWW 9.11). Read of Maria's experiences and be prepared to discuss the following questions.

1. How much money (in American dollars) does Maria earn in a week working at Maxell? How would this compare with a minimum wage job in the United States? How many hours do you have to work to earn enough money to buy a gallon of milk?

2. Why was Maria afraid to confront her employers about her wages and working conditions? How did her manager react to her complaints?

3. What do you see as the future for Maria's sons and Maria herself? Do you think her life is much different from women who work as food producers in Mexico – why?

PART TEN
COPING WITH A RAPIDLY CHANGING WORLD HUMAN INTERACTION WITH THE ENVIRONMENT

GOALS: As the great global warming debate rages, and El Niño is blamed for just about every great calamity on the planet, some areas are receiving too much precipitation and others not enough. The drought of 1998 will be long remembered by Texans as one of the most brutal and deadly on record. But while Texas was toasting, China was experiencing catastrophic floods. Are humans to blame for global climate change? Is there really anything such as "normal" weather conditions? Can humans continue altering the natural environment to suit their own needs without long-term effects? The following activities will focus on the challenge of humans versus the environment and the consequences of the perpetual tug of war.

ACTIVITIES: You will be studying the dynamics of human and environmental interfaces at a variety of scales. First, you will conduct an inventory of local water resources and examine specific water issues faced by your community. The second activity will turn students into time travelers to explore how variations in precipitation have changed the human experience and the natural environment. The final part of this section takes at look at the earth from a different perspective -- from space -- through remotely sensed satellite images. In this section, you will study a series of images and maps that illustrate landscape change resulting from human and natural processes.

Activity 10.1: Streams of Consciousness: Local Water Resource Issues

INTRODUCTION: Water plays an important role in every community. What would you do without fresh water? Often, the problem with water is that there is either too much or not enough and what water you do have may have quality problems. You may have enough water for now but future water needs could be a problem. Most of us take water for granted but that is a serious mistake. Have you ever given any thought as to water resources in your community? Explore your water world.

Activity 10.1 Field Work
Part A
Using a local map of your choosing, make an inventory all surface water resources in your local community. Begin with the largest streams and list the features in a hierarchy from largest to the smallest tributaries (include any bodies of water too).

1. What is the source of your community's municipal water?

2. Is this water used for any other purposes such as recreation, navigation, industry or irrigation?

3. Are there any local water uses you believe are "conflicts of interest" and if so, what are they and what could be done to mitigate the situation?

Part B

To access background information on water quality issues in your state, go to the "Regional U.S. Water Supply Problems" page at the *National Drought Mitigation Center* Web site (WWW 10.1). Compare your state's situation to that of other states in your region.

    1. How are the water problems in your state different or similar to the region?

    2. Are most of the water resource issues in your region more a result of the natural environment or of land use choices and economic activities by humans?

Part C

Look at Figure 32.2 in your text, "Variations in the Moisture Index in the United States." What is the moisture surplus or deficit for your location as indicated on the map? Compare these data with current conditions on the Web site for the *National Drought Mitigation Center*, using the current soil moisture map (WWW 10.2). Click on Current Standardized Precipitation Index Maps.

    1. What are the soil conditions for your region for the current month?

    2. How do the current soil precipitation index (SPI) conditions compare to the three-month, six-month, and 12-month data? Is your region experiencing drier, wetter, or unchanged conditions?

    3. What if any direct or indirect impacts of the SPI have you observed in your community -- for example, have there been any floods in your community over the past year or have drought conditions forced water usage restrictions?

Part D

Acid rain has many consequences not only for the points of origin, but also for those downwind who receive acidic rainfall. How many acid raindrops are falling on your head? To determine the pH of your local precipitation, go the *United States Environmental Protection Agency Acid Rain Program* page (WWW 10.3). First, click on What is Acidity and read what pH values represent. You should also read Acid Rain effects On Water before scrolling down to the bottom of the page and clicking on pH Map of the United States (1996). Find your location on the map and interpolate the pH value.

    1. Is your community's built or natural environment at risk for acid rain -- why or why not?

Activity 10.2: Highly Hydrological: Drought and Out in Basins and Hills

INTRODUCTION: Droughts and floods are a natural part of the climate system but human responses to such disasters vary as do the consequences. How we choose to cope with these calamities is based on scientific knowledge and cultural beliefs. For example, if you live in a floodplain, chances are, at some point in time you and your property will be at risk. Yet, we continue to live in hazardous locations and rebuild after a disaster, often on the same spot. In this activity, we will examine the causes and consequences of variations in precipitation which result in droughts.

Activity 10.2 Field Work
    Part A

We begin by visiting the *National Drought Mitigation Center* home page (WWW 10.4) and clicking on Why Plan?. Read through this section and as you progress, be sure to click on the following links within the article for more details: Impacts, List of Winners , Definition , Hydro-Illogical Cycle, Upper Missouri River Basin.

1. How do media-based meteorologists often mislead us into thinking there is such a thing as "normal weather?" Conversely, do you think weathercasters sensationalize "normal" weather extremes into news events? Can think of any examples from your local television stations?

2. How do National Drought Mitigation Center (NDMC) scientists view the relationship between drought and global warming? Do you agree or disagree with this assessment and why?

3. What are the four major defining categories for drought? Which economic activity is first affected by drought? Why is it so difficult for scientists to find a single definition for drought?

4. Who were the agricultural "winners" during the 1987-89 drought? How did energy and transportation sectors likewise benefit from the drought?

5. You know what the hydrologic cycle looks like from Figure 32.1 in your text, but what is the "hydro-illogical cycle?" Could this model also be applied to flooding -- why or why not?

6. How did drought effect the Upper Missouri River basin between 1987 and 1992? Which economic sectors were affected by the drought? How were irrigation and municipal water supplies compromised by the drought? What aspects of the natural environment suffered due to lower water levels? What role did the Army Corps of Engineers play in the decision making process? Why is this a good case study example of the hydro-illogical model?

Part B
Return to the *NDMC* home page (WWW 10.4) and click on <u>Impacts</u> then select <u>Coping and Recovering from Drought</u>. When you come to the part of this section on dust storms, follow this link to the *Discovery Channel Online's* "Day of the Black Blizzard" to travel back in time to the catastrophic drought of the 1920s and 1930s.

1. What are the "Dust Bowl Blues?" How did these "blues" weave their way into the "social fabric" of dust bowl communities? Why were sleeping pills in such great demand during this period?

2. Why were there so many jackrabbits during the dust bowl era?

3. How were the basic tasks of everyday life complicated by dust storms?

4. What brought about an end to the Dust Bowl era?

5. Is this region still prone to droughts and how did changes in precipitation amounts change peoples' perception of conservation programs?

6. What lessons have we learned from the Dust Bowl? Do you think the United States could experience a similar event today---why or why not?

Activity 10.3: Environmental Change As Viewed From Above
INTRODUCTION: Few images are more dramatic than those remotely sensed from satellites orbiting the earth. Even more important is to be able to compare land surface changes over time and interpret how human activities have altered the environment. The following activities are based on satellite images collected by the United States Geological Survey (USGS). Human-induced environmental change and its associated impacts are the foci. You will be asked to view satellite images and interpret the landscape change. Launch the USGS *Earthshots* Web site (WWW10.5), and be sure to view all the images for each year, zooming in and out when you can. Reference maps and photos are included with most images to assist in your orientation.

1. Garden City, Kansas

Garden City is used as an example to help orient you to the website. Please review all the links for Garden City so you can get the most out of each USGS image. If you are not familiar with remote sensing, this first site will be very helpful.

a. Think back to the Dust Bowl discussion in the previous section. What agricultural land use practice changes do you think have taken place in the Garden City area since the 1920s? What do the red circles represent on the image   could they be alien landing pads?

b. What is the Ogallala Aquifer and how has exploitation of this resource resulted in large-scale land use change? The Ogallala Aquifer is currently being depleted at a faster rate than it can be recharged. What do you think will happen to this region if the aquifer runs dry---are there any other water source alternatives?

2. Buraydah, Saudi Arabia

a. What specific agricultural land use practice do farmers in Buraydah have in common with those in Garden City?

b. What has enabled Saudi farmers to employ this particular practice and how is this different from the decisions made by farmers in Kansas?

3. Southern Mauritania

a. Take a look at Figure 32.5 in your text, "Areas Threatened by Desertification," and determine the risk factor for Mauritania. What evidence of desertification can you detect on the image for southern Mauritania between 1972 and 1990?

b. How have infrastructure developments added to the desertification problems?

c. What accounts for the bright red signatures indicating healthy growing vegetation near the town of Richard Toll? Do you think these crops are consumed locally or produced for export markets and why?

4. Phnom Penh, Cambodia

a. How would you translate "Phnom Penh" into English?

b. How do monsoonal rains alter the physical landscape and why do you think the 1985 image shows more surface water than the image for 1973?

c. Who is the Khmer Rouge and how did they change the demographic and landscape characteristics of the region?

d. Why were skilled professionals targeted for extermination by the Khmer Rouge and how did this in turn result in problems with the irrigation system?

5. Imperial Valley, California

a. How would you describe the Salton Sea and how was it formed?

b. How has irrigation changed the landscape of the Imperial Valley, both urban and rural?

6. Chernobyl, Ukraine

a. Why have three-headed cattails and increasing numbers of wildlife flourished in the area of the damaged Chernobyl nuclear power plant?

b. Compare the 1986 and 1992 images of Chernobyl. How do the colors of agricultural lands differ between the two time periods and what accounts for the vegetation changes?

6. Great Salt Lake, Utah

a. What does the Great Salt Lake have in common with the Salton Sea and how are the challenges faced by the region different from those in the Imperial Valley?

b. How are changing precipitation patterns threatening to make this the "Great Not-So-Salty

Lake?"

7. <u>Kara-Bogaz-Gol, Turkmenistan</u>
a. From a geopolitical point of view, would the KGB be worried about the KBG? In other words, how has the changing level of the Kara-Bogaz-Gol affected the political geography of Turkmenistan?

b. What do the Caspian Sea and the Great Salt Lake have in common?

c. How have changing levels of the Caspian Sea changed the physical and cultural landscapes in the region?

d. How have the changing water levels in the KBG and Caspian Sea affected the region's salt industry? How have salt production methods and transportation technology evolved over the past century?

8. <u>Aral Sea, Kazakstan</u>
You can compare these images to those in your text in Figure 32.3 "The Dying Aral Sea."

a. What are the major factors that have contributed to this incredible shrinking lake?

b. Has the health of Aral Sea area residents been affected by changes to the lake's ecosystem?

c. It has been said that "it's not nice to fool Mother Nature." Does the destruction of the Aral Sea lend credence to that expression---why or why not?

9. <u>Saloum River, Senegal</u>

a. What is a mangrove and what types of flora and fauna would you expect to find if you toured the Saloum River region?

b. Why are the mangroves experiencing environmental stress and how can this be detected from Landsat images?

10. <u>Rondônia, Brazil</u>
a. Deforestation can be as devastating as desertification as evidenced in this series of satellite images. Compare the images from 1975, 1986, and 1992. How would you describe the vegetation changes and why do "feathering" patterns emerge on the landscape?

b. Based on this series of images from Brazil, what do you think the Rondônia region will look like in another six years? What will be the environmental and human costs for Brazil and the world?

NOTES

NOTES

NOTES

NOTES

NOTES

NOTES

NOTES

NOTES

NOTES

NOTES

NOTES